THE TAROT
Art, Mysticism, and Divination

THE TAROT

Art, Mysticism, and Divination

by
Sylvie Simon

Inner Traditions International
Rochester, Vermont

Inner Traditions International, Ltd.
One Park Street
Rochester, Vermont 05767

This work was translated by Kit Currie and Sean Konecky

Copyright © 1986 by Editions Fernand Nathan

English translation copyright © 1988 by William S. Konecky Associates, Inc.

World English language rights reserved by William S. Konecky Associates, Inc.

All rights reserved. No part of this book may be reproduced or utilized in any form or by any means, electronic or mechanical, including photocopying and recording, or by any information storage and retrieval system, without permission in writing from the publisher. Inquiries should be addressed to Inner Traditions International, Ltd.

LIBRARY OF CONGRESS CATALOGING IN PUBLICATION DATA

Simon, Sylvie.
  The tarot.
  Translation of: Le tarot.
  Bibliography: p.
  Includes index.
  1. Tarot I. Title.
BF1879.T2S56 1988   133.3'2424   88-8957
ISBN 0-89281-216-8

10 9 8 7 6 5 4 3 2 1

Printed and bound in Spain.

Distributed to the book trade in the United States by Harper and Row Publishers, Inc.

Distributed to the book trade in Canada by Book Center, Inc., Montreal, Quebec.

Table of Contents

THE MAJOR ARCANA 9
  1. The Magician 10
  2. The High Priestess 12
  3. The Empress 16
  4. The Emperor 17
  5. The Hierophant 20
  6. The Lovers 24
  7. The Chariot 26
  8. Justice 28
  9. The Hermit 32
 10. The Wheel of Fortune 34
 11. Strength 35
 12. The Hanged Man 40
 13. Death 41
 14. Temperance 42
 15. The Devil 46
 16. The Tower 47
 17. The Star 48
 18. The Moon 49
 19. The Sun 50
 20. Judgment 52
 21. The World 53
The Fool 54

THE KEYS OF THE KINGDOM 11
Consciousness, Mirror of the Universe 11
"I Think, Therefore I Am" 11
Symbols Outside of Time 11
Past, Present, Future, at the Same Time 14
Is the Future Already Written? 15
By the Light of the Cards 21

WHERE DO THE CARDS COME FROM? . . . 23
The Appearance of Playing Cards in Europe . . . 23
Occultists' Tarots 24

A KABBALISTIC SCIENCE 31
The Tree of the Sephiroth 31
The Ten Sephiroth: Illumination and
  Divination 33
The Face Cards in the Tarot and the
  Hebrew Alphabet 43

THE MAJOR ARCANA SPEAK TO US 57
RELATIONSHIPS BETWEEN CARDS IN THE
  MAJOR ARCANA 57
METHODS OF READING 60
  Arrangement in the Form of a Cross 62
  Arrangement in a Row of Seven 62
  Arrangement in Three Rows of Three 63
  Arrangement by Astrological Houses 63

THE MINOR ARCANA 65
THE SUITS 65
  Swords 65
  Staves 65
  Cups 65
  Coins 66

THE FACE CARDS 66
  Kings 66
  Queens 71
  Knights 72
  Pages 74

THE NUMBERED MINOR ARCANA 76
 10. Message of Hope 76
  9. Initiation 80
  8. The Sword of Damocles 81
  7. The Holy Number 85
  6. Fluctuation and Hesitation 86
  5. Warlike Virtues 90

4. Solidity, Passivity 92	DIVINATIONS, AND CELEBRATED PROPHECIES FROM LEGEND AND HISTORY 115
3. Creation and Dynamism 94	
2. Dialogue 96	
1. The Ace—Absolute Consciousness 100	THE ORACLES OF ANTIQUITY 115
HOW TO READ THE MINOR ARCANA 102	DODONA AND DELPHI: HIGH PLACES OF THE ORACLES 115
	DIVINATION DURING THE RENAISSANCE 115
THE TAROT A SEEN BY ARTISTS AND POETS 107	*Nostradamus* 115
	Paracelsus 116
A Legion of Painters and Designers 107	*Mother Shipton: English Clairvoyant* 116
Poets Respond to the Call of the Tarot 107	*A Prediction Related by Saint-Simon* 116
	SEERS AND ASTROLOGERS OF THE EIGHTEENTH CENTURY 116
THE TAROT, MIRROR OF THE SOUL 109	
Man and Anxiety 110	*The Famous Prophecy of Cazotte* 118
Rememberance of Oneself 113	BIBLIOGRAPHY 119

*Two centers of interest, of reflection
intersect and form the basis for this book.
Not wanting to separate them we explore
these two intertwining themes in a simultaneous reading.*

*In reading or thumbing through this study
(curiosity is often the desire to grasp one's subject quickly)
the reader will discover from page 9 to page 55
bordered by rules in the colors of the Tarot of Marseilles:*

THE 22 MAJOR ARCANA
this is to say the cards that are the primordial path of divination

These are accompanied by a running text on:

THE POWERS

THE HISTORY, THE PHILOSOPHY

OF THE TAROT.

To Marcel Picard . . . Who Showed Me the Path of the Tarot

The Major Arcana

Wherein are described the twenty-two cards of the Major Arcana, with commentaries on their symbolism, relationship to the Bible, and esoteric tradition, and finally elucidation of their mysterious powers of divination.

The Magician

The first card of the major arcana, or greater secrets, in the tarot is the Magician. He sometimes bears the first letter of the Hebrew alphabet, *aleph*, whose intrinsic message is the unification of spirit and matter. He also represents the first Sephirah of the Tree of Life of the *Sepher Yezirah*, which has its origins in the Kabbalah, the esoteric teaching given to Moses by God. The Tree of the Sephiroth is a complex symbol representing the harmony of the cosmos and the soul of man in regard to that cosmos. The first Sephirah is Kesser, the crown, symbol of self-knowledge, of the spirit of the living God, the beginning of all things; it is the voice, the spirit, and the word. It is God, who creates and encompasses everything. The Kabbalah teaches that the One existed before any other number was born from it. It is indivisible and eternal, and it is the only number by which any other number can be multiplied without causing any change in value.

The *Tao Te Ching* tells us that "the one begat two, two begat three, three begat the whole human race." We find the same kind of affirmation in the words of Thoth, which may be read on the tomb of Petamon, priest of Amon in the Twenty-third Dynasty: "I am the one that becomes two, I am the two that becomes four, I am the four that becomes eight, but I am one who guards it."

The Kabbalah and Hermeticism adopted the point in the center of a circle as the representation of the one God, as the Hindus, Chinese, and wise men of the Middle Ages had done. Omar Khayyam, the great Persian poet of the twelfth century, wrote in one of his quatrains: "I pronounced the first letter of the alphabet and my heart said to me: now, I know. One is the first number of the innumerable."

The fathers of the Church considered One as the unity of God. The word *universe* means "turned to the One." The One is All, simple and infinite, a single unit and many. It is the symbol of the beginning and of the end. It is the emanation of heaven to earth.

Ramakrishna, the Brahmin sage of the nineteenth century, was more explicit: "Know the One and you know All." If zeros are added to one, it becomes millions; if one is taken away, nothing remains.

The Magician is also called Mage, Juggler, Minstrel, Sorcerer, Mountebank, Bagad, or Pagad. The card depicts a young man with fair, almost white hair, standing before a flesh-colored table, the color of matter. His left hand holds a yellow wand pointing upward, a sign of the evolution of matter; in his right hand is a gold coin, and this hand, pointing downward, represents the spirit penetrating matter. This first figure of the tarot stands for activity and energy, the creative principle in space. On his head is a wide-brimmed hat in the form of a lazy eight, a figure that stands for infinity in algebra and denotes boundless understanding. In front of him is a three-legged table (signifying the three pillars of the visible world, the absent fourth leg being the invisible world, and also recalling the three pillars of the temple of Solomon). On it we see a wallet in which to put the things in life that are to be kept, weights to measure and evaluate events, and dice representing chance. The knife symbolizes the power of the suit of swords; the money, the suit of coins (sometimes called pentacles); the goblet, the suit of cups; and the baton in his hand, the suit of staves. His feet, placed at right angles, are evocative of the balance of this thought and judgment; the tufts of grass are the unconscious behind the conscious. His Self is illimitable, but his knowledge is finite. He is the child of the Divine, but the seen universe is magic, and its vortex prevents us from seeing reality. The Magician is an illusionist whose foremost talent is his skill. He is creative, clever, and spontaneous. He can receive emanations from the earth, and because his feet are set at right angles, energy flows round him. He has all the requisites for success. This card always indicates good health and strong vitality. it is God alone who creates; he alone is real, and all else is illusion. If this card is badly placed it may indicate power used for unscrupulous ends, intrigue, deceit, greedy ambition, and even cheating.

The Magician represents man standing upright, and some anthropologists consider this as radical a distinction as man's reason. He is active, associated with the work of creation, and from him flows all manifestation, although the source is not apparent. He is energetic and creative, the beginning and end of all things, the revelation that elevates man by means of knowledge.

Thus, the Magician symbolizes spring, youth, the need for action, creative originality, self-confidence, craftsmanship, ambition, diplomatic ability, and the capacity to influence others.

The Keys of the Kingdom

It is stupidly presumptuous to disdain and condemn as untrue whatever does not seen probable to us. I used to do that at one time . . . If I spoke of prophecy or magic, I felt compassion for those poor people deluded by lunacy. Now, I find that I was just as much to be pitied.

—Montaigne

Consciousness, Mirror of the Universe

Since man first began to reflect upon the world in which he lives, he has been made uneasy by the Unknown that surrounds him, by the unforeseeable future, and by what his end will be, which he persists in trying to discover. He asks himself questions that he tries to answer by means of the most varied divinatory methods.

Very early in man's history, he sought to discover the fundamental principles of the cosmic order. If we acknowledge the order of the universe and the relationship between all its elements, we must also admit that chance does not exist, that everything is foreseen and arranged. Each thing is justified by the existence of all the others; each human being is interdependent with the universe as a drop of water is with the ocean. This idea was very well expressed by the Scottish poet James Thomson: "We cannot touch a flower without disturbing a star."

The idea according to which the structural design of the universe is contained in everything belonging to it was taken up by Teilhard de Chardin in *Le Groupe zoologique humain*: "In a single pine cone, or in a single artichoke leaf, we possess the whole structural law of fruits."

"I Think, Therefore I Am"

Descartes's famous axiom, formulated in his *Discourse on Method*, leads us to think that man, while a minuscule speck in the universe, is nevertheless the most highly evolved form of life because he has knowledge of his own existence. Self-knowledge, so dear to Socrates, brings the philosopher down from heaven to earth. On the pediment of the Temple of Delphi is written, "Know thyself." Philosophic tradition has added: "And you will know the universe and the gods."

The understanding of the universe is the departure point for all mystical experience, and all divination flows from this ability to reestablish the universe as a simple system of symbols that are both a miniaturization of it and its mirror.

The forerunner of the German metaphysicians, Jacob Boehme (1575–1624), stated that man must see and comprehend himself what the exterior world is: It is a microcosm in the macrocosm of the universe.

Symbols Outside Time

Symbols were born at the same time as human thought. Ever since man first began to reflect, he could escape with the help of certain symbols, the archetypes. Philo of Alexander speaks of them, as do Irenaeus and Denis the Areopagite. Saint Augustine did not use the same word, but he took up its meaning.

Later C. G. Jung was to find in man's spirit, at the limits of knowledge, a region he called the personal unconscious. This unconscious contains private memories, things once known but now fallen into oblivion and sometimes voluntarily repressed by the person. Even more profoundly buried under this seemingly superficial layer is the collective unconscious, which has no location in space or time but which extends through space and time so that it appeared to Jung like an ever-present continuum, a universal presence unencompassed. This unconscious does not receive personal imagery, but only that common to all men—the archetypes.

These primordial images are a kind of universal memory, a patrimony transmitted by heredity but not known to the subject, representing forgotten myths, lost traditions, ancestral religions with their gods and demons, the fundamental experiences of the human race. Before Jung, man knew nothing of this invisible kingdom over which he reigns unconsciously.

The High Priestess

Sometimes called the Papess, the High Priestess is seated on a throne, calm, silent, impassive, mysterious, in contrast to the Magician, who is lively and expressive. She does not promulgate her teachings; she waits for people to seek her out.

Her blue cloak, the color of spirituality, hides the strength and vitality represented by her red dress. She wears the three-tiered papal crown, that of the initiate who holds the Book of Wisdom in her hands. This is the Book of Books, the book of the Dies Irae (Day of Wrath). Some see in this book the symbol of the tarot. In any case it is the Book of Secrets, which should not be revealed to those who are not ready to hear.

Behind the Priestess is the colored veil of materialism, which hides the entrance to the door of the Temple, the sacred precinct. It is the veil that prevents the profane from entering into the Holy of Holies, the veil that was rent from top to bottom when the heavens were obscured at the death of Christ. It also reminds us of the veil of Isis. Plutarch tells us that written on the statue of Isis at Sais are the words "I am all that has been, that is, and that will be, and no mortal has ever dared to lift my veil."

Temples are a reflection of the divine world; they are earthly replicas of the celestial archetypes. Thus, Buddhist temples have a horizontal structure like the mandala, representing the cosmos. The temple is a reduction of the macrocosm and a likeness of the microcosm. It is at the same time the world and man, and symbolizes the way to enlightenment.

The High Priestess does not raise the veil that hides the doors of the secret sanctuary, for man by himself must seek and find truth. Buddha teaches that men may be shown the way of truth but that they must traverse it themselves. Isis, the supreme and universal goddess, the source and beginning of existence, is the initiator who withholds all the secrets of life, death, and resurrection.

The High Priestess knows that there exists another world beyond our knowledge, beside our earthly universe. There are the outside material world and the spiritual interior world, united beyond matter. They cannot exist without each other, like the yang and yin, whose two poles are in God from whom was born the Word, the first creator.

The High Priestess, who may be compared to Juno, goddess of marriage and procreation, as well as to the Sphinx, knows the answer to the questions men ask themselves: "Whence do we come? Who are we? Where are we going?" We might remember here that these three questions are to be found on one of Paul Gauguin's most arcane Tahitian pictures.

The High Priestess is always connected with the letter *beth*, the second in the Hebrew alphabet. She is the first test for man; he must be accepted by her in order to arrive at knowledge. The *Zohar* (see p. 31) teaches us that when the letters of the alphabet appeared before God—the En Soph of the *Sepher Yezirah*—so that he could create the world, he chose *beth* as the foundation. *Beth* begins *bereshit*, first word of the Bible, which for Jews is the book that contains the Torah, the Law. *Beth* presided over the creation of the world. She is the keeper of the secrets of Genesis. She receives, whereas *aleph* emits. She corresponds to Chochmah, the second Sephirah of the Tree of Sephiroth, representing Wisdom, passivity, stability.

The High Priestess bears the number 2, the first even number, therefore embodying the feminine principle. Here God, as creative principle, gives us our first idea of otherness. One in itself cannot think, because to think is to distinguish and compare things.

According to Plotinus, understanding when it thinks must be double. Duality teaches us that what is below is like that which is above, and vice versa. The binary principle is tied to the idea of alternation—day and night; summer and winter; light and darkness; heaven and hell; good and evil; the yin passive, feminine, and black; and the yang active, masculine, and white. Without this duality there is no exertion and therefore no creation; in opposites lies fertility.

The High Priestess symbolizes teaching, authority, understanding, wisdom, clairvoyance, the priesthood, religious and metaphysical knowledge, morality, goodwill, intelligence, but also the idea of strictness and duty.

In matters of health, this card may indicate hidden illness, fever, organic problems—especially of a genital nature—epidemics, tumors, and above all, pregnancy.

Generally it represents elderly women, and more than anything it stands for the originator of things, fertile Mother Nature. She is contemplative, presiding over reading and writing, literature, and the occult.

She is the womb from which all beings come, the return to our origins, the most mysterious card in the tarot.

The High Priestess, associated with *beth*, the second letter of the Hebrew alphabet, bears the number 2, the first even number, standing for the feminine principle, the womb of living beings. 1. The High Priestess of the Visconti-Sforza tarot, a likeness of Sister Manfreda, kinswoman of the Visconti family, and elected papess by a religious Lombard sect, the Guglielmites. She wears the habit of the Humiliati. 2. In the Besançon tarot, the High Priestess has yielded place to Juno, as the Pope to Jupiter, in order not to frighten the believers. (From a set designed c. 1750 by the master playing-card maker Jean-Pierre Laurent, at Belfort; Musée des Arts et Traditions populaires.) 3. The High Priestess of a Parisian tarot deck (seventeenth century, Bibliothèque nationale.)

In the Visconti-Sforza tarot, the World is one of the major arcana from the brush of Antonio Cicognaro. The majority of the other cards were painted by Bonifacio Bembo. Perhaps the fortified city, pounded by waves, represents the heavenly city of Jerusalem. The most auspicious of the tarot cards, the World is at the same time a summing up and an end: Is not number 21 (3 × 7) the number of perfection in the Bible?

Images of the past, but also of eternity, these archetypes are universal, appearing in all mythologies. They illustrate the "forms of behavior" in all situations that spring from them. Independent of physical space or time, they make it easier for thought to move in space-time.

Past, Present, Future at the Same Time

"The subconscious has no grounds for being localized in the present as the conscious has, but if it is temporally extended, it is towards the future. It is in this sense that the past and the future both exist." All relativist authors agree with Olivier Costa de Beauregard; he is echoed by the famous mathematician Hermann Weyl: "The world does not simply become; it is." It is past, present, and future at the same time. Human psychism can stretch itself along the entire space-time continuum. Bergson saw the unconscious reaching toward the past, but relativity obliges us to think of it also as in the future—the past and future cannot be disassociated in this continuum.

The divinatory arts allow us to transcend space-time and to enter what is outside earthly time for a little while.

Since in physics all particles can move forward or back equally in time, as they can go right or left in space, there is no reason to consider that time flows in only one direction, from the past into the future.

Louis de Broglie, like many modern physicists, joins with eastern philosophy when he expresses the idea that everything in space-time that constitutes past, present, and future for all of us is all of a piece, and each observer discovers in the course of time new sections of space-time that appear successively ordered in the material world, while in reality all the occurrences of space-time exist before we have knowledge of them.

For his part, D. T. Suzuki, the Buddhist philosopher, claims that in the spiritual world no such divisions of time as past, present, and future exist, because they are reabsorbed into a single present moment in which existence vibrates with its true meaning. The past and future are both mixed in this present instant of enlightenment, for in the absolute there is no time or space. Dogen, one of the masters of Japanese Zen Buddhism, had already expressed this idea in the thirteenth century, in a different way, but one that fits in with modern scientific experiments: "Most people think that time passes; in fact, it stays where it is." The idea that it flows is illusory.

There is no universal flight of time, as was believed

for so long, but since only its passing is visible, we find it hard to understand that it stays where it is. "Time, that moving image of motionless eternity," as J. B. Rousseau wrote. But in reality, it is time that is motionless and the dynamic universe that moves in continual expansion. Time is immutable; there is no before and no after.

Space-time is an infinite space in which all occurrences are interrelated. We wrongly believe that we see these at the moment when they happen. Observers moving at different speeds will place events differently in time. All measurements of space and time are therefore subjective and have no absolute meaning. Likewise in quantum mechanics, the only possible interpretation of phenomena is one is which the observer plays a role in the phenomenon observed.

Light needs a certain amount of time to move from the place where something has happened to the spot where it may be observed. This interval is generally too short to be perceptible to most of us, but it is different in astronomy, where the distances are considerable. Light takes eight minutes to reach us from the sun, so we see that star as it was eight minutes earlier. This phenomenon is accentuated when we observe objects farther from the solar system. The nearest star appears to our eyes after a four-year lag, and some galaxies have aged several million years in the interval before the light from them reaches us.

All these apparently complex ideas are necessary if we are to understand that our thought can, for a brief earthly moment, enter that definite "elsewhere" that is space-time. Perception travels along the trajectory unfolded before it.

We can illustrate these scientific considerations on time very simply if we take the example of the flight of an airplane. Before it appears to an observer it is in the future; when it passes overhead it is in the present to him, and it quickly disappears into the past. But for the plane or for another that may follow it, all three moments are in the present.

Is the Future Already Written?

That is the great debate between freedom and determinism. If the future is already written, who wrote it? Is it God or man himself who creates by thinking the events that will mark his life?

It is the totality of our actions that influences our destiny. Taoism teaches that if man acts according to intuitive wisdom, if he remains in continuous harmony

As painted by Bembo, the Hermit holds an hourglass instead of the lantern seen in many tarot decks. Thus, he is associated here not with Diogenes, but with Chronos, the Saturn of the Romans, the Father of Time eating up the years. His blue gown, the color of spirituality, indicates passion controlled. The Hermit exhorts us to prudence, to meditation, and to reflection upon true hidden values.

The Empress

The Empress is the first figure of the tarot who is shown full face. She smiles serenely. She is Athena of the Greeks and Minerva of the Romans, privileged daughter of Jupiter, sprung from the brain of her father, goddess of war, sciences, and arts. Like the High Priestess, she is seated on a flesh-colored throne that represents matter: She understands man's problems. The blue of her tunic stands for the spirit, which her red dress converts into energy. Her headdress is also red, indicating mental action, the interior activity from which intelligence is born; she is crowned with gold, the sign of divine love.

Her wings allow her to soar to the summits of universal intelligence. This is realized by human and earthly means, but her mind is able to attain the Absolute.

Her scepter shows us that she rules the three worlds—heaven, earth and the world between. She holds it in her left hand, and she rules therefore with the passive force of the eternal feminine. The scepter is surmounted by a globe and a cross, alchemical symbol of antimony, or the state close to perfection, which awaits only the passing of the final stage to be transformed into absolute perfection or complete failure.

On the shield in her right hand we see a yellow or gilded eagle, the color of eternity. The eagle is a symbol of heaven and the sun, the bird of Zeus and of Saint John the Evangelist. It is the bird of light and represents the sun, fire, the father, and virility; it is brave and courageous but also proud, rapacious, and cruel. It occupies an important place in the mantic or divinatory practice; the augurs interpret its flight. Both Hindus and Native Americans attribute supernatural power to it and adorn themselves with its feathers. Shamans often wear eagle wings.

Whereas the High Priestess remains hidden and secret, the Empress is open and luminous. She addresses herself to all men who seek truth. The High Priestess is the paramour, the Empress is the wife. The High Priestess is the unconscious; the Empress, the conscious. Thanks to her scepter she reigns over time and matter. Her energy creates everything that intelligence can grasp; she unites matter and spirit, still separate in the High Priestess. By this union she makes the divine become human and teaches man that if he puts his spirit and soul to rights, he will stay healthy and well balanced.

The Empress uses her body as a precious instrument in the service of her spirit, of which it is only a distant manifestation. She knows that Creation is one and indivisible.

The Empress represents the third Sephirah, Binah, creative intelligence, and the letter *gimel* in the Hebrew alphabet, material manifestation of spiritual ideas and creative energy, as well as of the fruits of the marriage of that energy with the earth. The Empress is the mother of imagery, of ideas, the immaculate Virgin, and Venus, queen of heaven.

She symbolizes harmonic realization, the driving force, all the opulence of femininity. She is also the balanced mind, the businesswoman, mother, sister, spouse, the practical woman who is decisive, intuitive, and fascinating. Her mind is free and lucid. She is careful, calm, serene, and intellectual. When badly placed she may indicate infidelity, inconstant love, vanity, pretense. Embodying the desire for knowledge, she is interested in psychoanalytical research and in witticisms. She indicates disorders of the head, both physical and psychic.

She carries the number 3, fundamental and holy, considered the most perfect number by the ancients. The fact that a name or an invocation was repeated three times made it holy.

Lao-tsu teaches in the *Tao Te Ching* that three engenders all things. In *Timaeus* Plato says, "It is quite impossible to combine two things without a third, for there must be a bond that binds them." And in his *Treatise on Heaven* Aristotle says, "There is no other greatness than that because 3 includes all possible things."

2 is the number of the earth, 3 is that of heaven. It is the universal basic number. For Christians, the consummation of divine unity is three persons in one Godhead. The divine manifestation is three-fold in most religions, as time is three-fold (past, present, and future), and as the theological virtues are, and the elements of the Great Work of alchemy—sulphur, salt, and mercury.

Life has three aspects: birth, living, and death; there are three divine activities: creation, conservation, destruction; three aspects of time: past, present, and future; three states of consciousness: heaven, earth, and hell.

The Empress is the queen of the world, she is animated and higher intelligence, the active principle, judgment, and she is also counselor.

The Emperor

The Emperor is seated in profile on a throne of an earthen color. He stares with single-minded purpose upon a road completely laid out for him. He has a distant air that seems to lose itself on a mysterious horizon and the stern demeanor of a guide who watches over the fulfillment of destiny. He does not judge; he guides the world. His beard is a token of his power and wisdom.

He is the first personage of the tarot to wear a blue garment under a red jacket. The red that covers his arms shows that action waits upon his intelligence, controlled by the blue of his mind. These two forces pervade the material world of which the Emperor is the uncontested ruler.

His red cap indicates his victorious intellectual activity; his yellow or golden crown is his faculty of manifesting his spiritual power by word and thought. He embodies all the potentiality that the Empress carried in herself. His absolute sovereignty is confirmed by the triangular points of his helmet, which is thus enabled to receive cosmic influences and which covers the nape of his neck, a particularly sensitive place on a man.

In his right hand he holds the scepter of power and the globe of universal domination. On the shield by his feet is the Emperor's eagle, which is ready to take flight and looks to the left; it is connected with the depths of the earth and looks in the opposite direction in order to ensure the balance of power by the opposition of contrary forces. His hand on his belt asserts his authority and defends him from bad influences, as his crossed legs retain favorable forces and keep less favorable ones away.

His throne, often called the cubic stone, represents immutable stability. The Emperor wears a green medallion, and he is therefore impressionable to emotions, unlike the Empress. In her, innate intelligence can lead to wisdom; in him, wisdom commands intelligence. Between the two they personify the masculine, positive and the feminine, negative aspects of a single divine unity. The sum of their numbers (3 + 4) equals 7, the key number of the terrestrial level.

The Emperor reigns over the actual; he ennobles himself in carrying out the plan of the Great Architect of the Universe, thanks to the power that comes from his soul and his high aspirations. He is the Demiurge of Platonic philosophy, which constructs the world and man. He is Jupiter of the Romans, Zeus of the Greeks, god of wisdom and ruler of the material world. Jupiter sets off thunder, lightning, and thunderbolts.

According to tradition, the Emperor is in harmony with the Great Bear, where humanity's teachers are. He is interested in spiritual questions, but with him, action outweighs reflection, intelligence and power triumphing only when they can manifest themselves. He does not keep his experiences to himself.

He represents authority, maturity, self-confidence, power, realization, virility, competence, will, reason, observation, exactitude, sternness, decision, constructive work, harmony, solid foundations. He is a man of business, father, spouse, and brother.

His reign is not brutal. He dominates by intelligence, reason, and affection; he is ready to serve as a guide, to be the connecting link between man and the higher powers. He is also a counselor.

Badly placed, he can indicate a redoubtable adversary, obstinacy, despotism, the abuse of power reaching tyranny, hostility.

He indicates good health, soundness, and resistance but sometimes in an excessive amount. He also stands for the neck, the shoulders, and the throat.

His number is 4, which suggests the square and the cube, therefore volume, which itself gives the idea of matter. According to Philo, number 4 is the first number to show the nature of a solid.

In the Bible, the number 4 introduces the concept of universality: the four horsemen of the Apocalypse, the four evangelists, the four elements, the four cardinal points, the four phases of the moon, the four seasons, the four letters of the divine name.

According to the tradition of the Sufis, the neophyte must pass four doors, which represent the four elements. For C.G. Jung, "Quaternity represents the archetypical foundation of the human psyche." The conscious mind has four fundamental functions—thought, perception, intuition, and feeling.

Four is a passive number, even, feminine, all qualities that the ancients attributed to earth.

The fourth letter of the Hebrew alphabet, associated with the Emperor, is the letter *daleth*, which signifies the Door. When *daleth* went before God beside the letter *gimel*, He enjoined that they never be separated because each nurtured the other. The Emperor is always linked with the Empress; they are complementary.

The Hierophant

The Hierophant (sometimes called the Pope) is a somewhat older bearded man, the first figure of the tarot seated not on flesh-colored matter, but on a white throne, signifying purity, his rule is therefore occult. He is more spiritual than his predecessors, which is also indicated by his white arms, a sign of wisdom operating in the temporal realm.

Like the High Priestess, he is an initiator. He knows secrets, but he imparts them, while she waits for them to be sought out: There is no veil behind him, for he has nothing to hide. He always has a yellow glove, which confirms the heavenly origin of his power. He bears the Templar cross, proof that he addresses himself to the initiated.

The Hierophant is clothed like the High Priestess, the blue of his robe, thanks to his red cloak, projecting his wisdom and love onto those whom he blesses. His tiara, sign of spirituality and supreme authority, and his scepter with three horizontal crossbars show that he reigns on three planes—physical, intellectual, and divine.

Seated between the two blue columns that mark the passage from one world to the next, he siphons off their energies. The verticality of the columns confirms man's elevation to God They connect with the Tree of Life, which contains the alphabet, the Tree of the World, which joins the earth to heaven. The column represents the knowledge that turns the soul toward perfection.

The Hierophant rules by balancing men's inclinations until they are in harmony. He is the High Priest who works in the material world but remains spiritual, devoting his energies to helping others. He is full of indulgence toward human frailty. His passions have abated, leaving a calm lucidity. He is a man of pardon and pity.

He directs himself toward two categories of the faithful, represented by the two kneeling neophytes before the pontifical throne. The size of these two figures is disproportionately reduced in order to emphasize better the majestic grandeur of the Hierophant, who counsels and adapts religious knowledge to the needs of believers. He is a lighthouse shining on the city and the world. He gives his blessing to these persons, but he does not direct them.

The Hierophant symbolizes moral and spiritual evolution, order, self-control, benevolence, the Word, physical maturity, experience, spiritual power operating in the temporal realm, goodness, mental balance, ability to synthesize, pity, religion, and intuitive philosophy.

Badly placed, he can indicate a certain conformity, conservatism, dissimulation, rancor, superstition, pride, bigotry, fanaticism, and intolerance.

He is a good medical counselor.

He is associated with the letter *he*, the fifth in the Hebrew alphabet and signifying that life is created and expressed by the breath of the divine. It is the Word that allows self-knowledge. If 5, the number of the Hierophant, is added to 2, that of the High Priestess, we get the same result as the addition of the Emperor's number, 4, and that of the Empress, 3. The number 7 was for Saint Augustine the perfection of fullness.

The Hierophant's number, 5, is the number of Christ, of the Word, of Man. *Logos*, the Word, divides the divine number 10 into two equal and effective parts to obtain the number of man, who has five fingers, five senses. Man is constructed like a five-pointed star and inscribes himself in a pentagram.

In Islam, the pentagram means marriage. It originates from a Chinese ideogram that represents man stretched out, arms and legs at right angles, his sexual organ being the center and his limbs and torso the points.

5 is the manifestation of man at the end of biological and spiritual evolution. According to Plutarch, when we add 2, the first even feminine number, and 3, the odd masculine number, we get 5, the result of their union. Being uneven it indicates an action and not a state. It is the middle of the first nine numbers and therefore holds them together.

The Pythagoreans considered 5 the nuptial number. For them 4 signified the body, inasmuch as matter is composed of four elements, but 5 was the body in its perfect form. This five-sided harmony, dear to the Pythagoreans, inspired the architecture of the Gothic cathedrals.

Paracelsus taught that the most powerful of all signs, that of the microcosm, was the pentagram. The pentacle is employed as a talisman. When its point is directed upward it unites with heaven; directed downward it joins the infernal forces.

The rose of the Rosicrucians has five petals.

The Hierophant represents above all union, conciliation, transmission, the marriage of the earthly and heavenly principles. He teaches us what is advisable for us to know.

with the world that surrounds him, his actions will succeed as long as they are in accord with the divine plan. We come to the free will of which Origen, the philosopher and theologian, wrote in the third century, in his treatise *De Principis:* "Rational beings themselves have the faculty of free will. The exercise of this faculty has drawn some to develop their will in imitation of God, others to weaken it by negligence. Such is the cause of diversity among rational beings. It does not come from the wish or judgment of the Creator, but from the free will of each man."

However, free will seems very limited: Great events are written and determined, and our free will resides only in the way we live them. Some individuals sustain the ordeal better than others, in the midst of misfortune rejoicing in a friendly gesture, in a ray of sunshine, while others, who appear to have all they need to be happy, refuse to see the good fortune offered to them.

Free will is the indeterminable factor that leaves man a certain choice. He experiences this freedom with his limited consciousness (consciousness means "to know the whole").

This idea of implacable fate was in evidence in the Greek theater, where tragic heroes had to confront an often cruel destiny. They chose their way freely, however, even when they knew it would lead them to disaster. Thus Oedipus, the hero shared by three great Greek dramatists, Sophocles, Aeschylus, and Euripides, chose freely; it was not the gods or fate that caused his ruin, but himself alone, by his will, by his loyalty to the Thebans. His choice was in accord with a doom he could not escape, despite the oracle's warning. Each of his decisions brought him irreparably nearer to the fatal fulfillment of the prophecy, in all its horror and apparent absurdity. But the unavailing struggle of the heroes of tragedy raises them above everyday mediocrity and allows them to fulfill themselves while remaining faithful to their honor and to their sense of justice and greatness. Finally, what determines our destiny is not events but what we make of them.

Pythagoras wrote that "the evils that beset men are the results of their choices, for they seek afar the fortune of which they bear the fruits."

The preceding pages show the manufacturing of playing cards in Paris, in the Place Dauphine in the seventeenth century. The outlines of the designs were drawn on woodblocks, then the background excised before inking. After printing was completed, the cards were colored by hand or stencil. Then they were separated. (Musée Carnavalet.)

By the Light of the Cards

Among the many ways of reading this already written future, the tarot is the easiest to learn for those who do not possess any exceptional gifts of divination. The tarot cards light up psychic images that may arise in a state of meditation—even a superficial one—and that produce in us a sort of internal illumination.

These images, connected to the magical art of invocation, activate the creative forces of our psyche and cause the emergence into our conscious mind of those powers drawn from the collective unconscious. They animate our sensory perceptions, our instincts and intuitions. These symbols, these archetypes, awaken in us sleeping or unrevealed knowledge, from the most secret depths of our unconscious. We must allow these symbols to operate until images suddenly emerge through which our intuition can recognize our internal experience in its outward aspect.

The tarot contains the cosmic plan; it therefore contains knowledge of the future. In order to extract this knowledge, one must observe the tarot cards; then one will see the psychic image of one's "self." The meaning of each card must be learned and its relations with its neighbors discovered in order to decipher the written future.

The arcana can be regarded as the antennae of the soul. This sensitivity was described by Goethe: "[We] can project these antennae beyond corporal limits and we can then have a presentiment or even a real intuition of our future."

When we choose one card over another, our carnal soul guides our choice, helped by our spiritual soul. Since the cards have the advantage of hiding their meaning until they are turned over, our conscious mind cannot influence our unconscious.

The symbols of the tarot describe degrees of knowing in the macrocosm and the microcosm. Man must change in order to alter his destiny. In order to educate himself about his true nature, he must get rid of the errors that cloud his understanding.

The tarot helps in the attainment of the consciousness that helps to control one's destiny. Nevertheless, we will be able to know only what we are allowed to know. Shadowy regions in prophecy guarantee us a margin of freedom. A certain mystery is necessary; otherwise, we would have neither hope nor desire. A life of which too much is known in advance loses the charm of being lived. Happily for us, our potential for choice is almost infinite; we can play the game according to our own tastes. Facing the same fate with the same qualities, two people may act completely differently. In that lies a great mystery and also a great hope.

Where Does the Tarot Come From?

There are two kinds of divination: one comes from art, the other from nature.

—Cicero, *De Divinatione*

No one knows whether the tarot originated in the East or in Europe, but much literature exists on its genesis. It has been suggested that the cards were first drawn by the Chinese, the Hindus, the Koreans, or even by the Chaldeans, the Hebrews, the Greeks, and the pre-Columbian Indians; some authors do not hesitate to place them even further back in history, attributing them to the Egyptians in the time of the Pharaohs. Almost every imaginable theory has been put toward at one time or another.

In actuality, we find the first traces of playing cards in China in the tenth century. In an encyclopedia it is noted that the Emperor Mu Tsung knew of them in 969.

The Appearance of Playing Cards in Europe

In Europe we must wait until the year 1367 in Berne to find a prohibition on playing cards among some legal documents, followed by a similar ban in Florence in 1376. Three years later in Belgium Renier Hollander, the receiver general of Brabant, laid out four peters and two florins to buy a deck for the prince of Brabant. In 1397, the provost of Paris forbade workmen to play at cards, except on feast days.

The introduction of playing cards into Europe apparently dates from this time. Would not the absence of earlier passages than these indicate that the cards were unknown before this in Europe? In any case, toward the end of the fourteenth century mentions of their existence multiply. But these are references to cards and not to the tarot, and we do not know what the cards looked like.

In the account book of Charles Poupart, silversmith to King Charles VI, we find that in 1392 he paid Jacquemin Gringonneur fifty-six Parisian sous for three decks of gilded cards, painted for the king. It was long thought that this set of cards was the one kept at the Bibliothèque nationale in Paris, but it now seems certain that this latter, very large and hand painted, dates back only to the middle of the fifteenth century and is of Venetian origin. Nevertheless, it is still known as the Tarot of Jacquemin Gringonneur. Seventeen cards remain from it that bear neither numbers, letters, nor inscriptions but whose symbols resemble those of the modern tarot.

The pack includes sixteen major arcana and one Page of Swords, leading us to think that it was originally a complete set composed of twenty-two major arcana, or trump cards, and fifty-six minor arcana, from which are derived our modern playing cards (which have only fifty-two cards after the suppression the knights). The pack called Gringonneur was bequeathed to the king of France in 1711 by Roger de Gaignières, tutor to the grandchildren of Louis XIV.

Undoubtedly the oldest tarot deck known is that painted for the Visconti-Sforza family, which ruled in Milan from the thirteenth to the fifteenth centuries. There are three packs extant, all incomplete but of exceptional quality. The oldest of the three sets, which appeared over a matter of some years, was probably executed in 1428 for the marriage of Bianca-Maria Visconti with Francisco Sforza. The arms of the Visconti family, which were then taken over by Francisco Sforza, are recognizable on some cards. These large cards are hand painted and richly illuminated.

The tarocchi packs of Mantegna exist in two examples that date from around 1470 but seem to have been copied from an older edition. Made up of fifty cards, of which the illustrations are derived from classical gods and astrological symbols, this set bears an indisputable resemblance to the tarot but cannot really be considered as such, while the symbols of the Visconti-Sforza cards are very similar to modern tarots.

The *minchiates* are of the ninety-seven-card variety of tarot. They are of Florentine origin and date from the

Opposite page: The Fool from the tarot deck of Charles VI. It is one of seventeen cards preserved at the Bibliothèque nationale that were for a long time ascribed to Jacquemin Gringonneur, from whom the king's silversmith had commissioned them. But today it is thought that these cards, handpainted like those of the Visconti-Sforza, are of Venetian origin.

The Lovers

The Lovers card shows a young man standing between two women. One is young, blonde, and smiling; she is dressed in blue, signifying sweetness, spirituality, pure and platonic love; her sleeves are white. However, the young man is looking with interest at the older woman dressed in red; she is less beautiful but more active and energetic. She grasps him by the shoulder to turn him toward herself. The young man is the Magician, whose hat has disappeared and who stands at the crossroads of his destiny, each foot pointing in an opposite direction, a sign of his indecision.

Having now become the Lover, he hesitates between Vice, who gives him a glimpse of an easy life, and Virtue, who does not hide from him the struggle he will have on the difficult way of the spirit. He hesitates because he has trouble resisting temptation. One must know temptation in order to understand those who have stumbled on this path and offer them a helping hand.

Saint Anthony underwent temptation of the flesh as well as the spirit while he slept. Jesus himself was tempted by Satan in the Garden of Olives. Every man who is born finds himself someday at a crossroads, in doubt as to his choice, tempted by the easy way that may be offered him.

Saint Matthew gives us counsel about the two roads: "Enter ye in by the strait gate: for wide is the gate and broad is the way, that leadeth to destruction, and many there be which go in thereat; because strait is the gate and narrow is the way, which leadeth unto life, and few there be that find it."

The white sun, emblem of purity, dispenses with its colored rays those energies that will guide and help the male lover to choose his destiny. He is barefoot so that he may sense the terrestrial forces. Cupid, representing human love, carries a stringless bow; thus the arrow he points toward the Lovers is purely symbolic. This arrow is charged with the emotion that will lead the male lover to choose one or other of the two women and the two roads before him. Will he pursue the steep slope of initiation, or will he let himself be carried away by ease and smoothness with the risk of having to go back along the road already traveled to find himself again at the point of departure?

With this card we find ourselves in the conscious world. It can be interpreted in two ways, through emotion or through experience. It urges us to know ourselves, to make a constructive synthesis after a choice. This card poses a problem between determinism and free will, similar to that of ambivalence and irresolution due to lack of experience.

Equally, it indicates a sentimental meeting, a new idyll, as well as freedom of choice, temptation. It can also indicate putting something to the test, indecision, uncertainty, dissatisfaction, lack of maturity, a fear of failing the test. Sometimes it indicates unfaithfulness, instability, and inconstancy.

It is the card of good health, of care by gentle and natural methods, and of the choice of a treatment.

It corresponds to the Hebrew letter *vav*, the fastener or hook that binds things together; it is a symbol of union and fecundity that bind heaven and earth.

The Lovers corresponds also to the sixth Sephirah of the Kabbalah, Tiphares, that Beauty which Plato says "awakens the desire for the eternal in men." So this arcanum also symbolizes the arts, such as painting and the cinema.

It bears the number 6, of which Saint Augustine says, "God created the world in six days because that is the perfect number." From that we get the two following theosophic operations: $1 + 2 + 3 = 6$ and $1 \times 2 \times 3 = 6$. Six is divisible by each of those numbers.

It is an even number, feminine and passive. It is also the six-pointed star formed by two triangles. The one whose point is up represents the holy Trinity, the other whose point is down represents the material world. Man must join his earthly body to his divine self.

The six-pointed star stands for the heart of man; this star is the Seal of Solomon, that wise and just king who built his temple on six points and whose throne had six steps.

The hexagon is an unusual figure because the radius of the circle inscribed within it is the same length as one side of the six equilateral triangles that divide the figure. Solomon's Seal is for man the memory of the earthly paradise and the Fall. It is the star of the macrocosm, the union of the human soul and the divine spirit; it is also the shield of David, the emblem of Israel. It always expresses the conjunction of two opposites, a principle and its reflection.

The Lovers means reconciliation and the contrary, antagonism. It means also the transitory world between the spirit and matter that leads us to unity by way of love.

beginning of the sixteenth century. It is possible that their imagery was partly inspired by the celebrated poem of Petrarch *I Trionfi*, for we find its symbols on many of the major arcana.

In the fifteenth century, the word *trionfi* was used in Italy to designate the twenty-two major arcana. The word *tarocchi* (plural of *tarocco*) was not used until the beginning of the following century, and always to describe the twenty-two major arcana. Later, this term encompassed the complete deck of cards with the major arcana augmented by the fifty-six minor arcana. *Tarot* then derives from an Italian word. *Arcanum*, which designates the symbolism of the cards, comes from the Latin *arcanus*, meaning mystery.

In 1500, we find in the manuscript *Sermones de Ludo cum Alis* a complete list of the major arcana with their names and numbers as used today, but some are in different order. The tarot of Catelin Geoffroy, made at Lyons in 1557, is the first deck to have the arcana enumerated in their current order.

The number of different tarots increased in Italy to the end of the seventeenth century, including that of Venice, or the Piedmont tarot, and the tarot of Bologna among many others.

Etteilla, from his real name of Alliette, was a wigmaker who told fortunes. He designed his own tarot deck, modifying the usual imagery, but the first twenty-one numbered cards and the last one (numbered 78) more or less represent the major arcana.

The tarot of Marseilles, whose imagery is much older, was designed at the end of the seventeenth century, inspired by a tradition dating back long before that; many variants are clearly inspired by the Middle Ages. It is impossible to know whether the Marseilles tarot came from a single source or whether it was born from successive transformations. Except for the head-to-tail figures, the cards are always close to those of the Piedmont tarot. One of the oldest sets was published in 1701 by Jean Dodal. Those generally found for sale were originally done by Nicolas Conver, master papermaker at Marseilles, in 1761.

Occultists' Tarots

Since their first appearance the tarot cards had been a game as well as a means of foretelling the future, but until the end of the fifteenth century, they were used exclusively at court, remaining a privilege of the aristocracy. With the invention of printing they became more common. The outlines of the figures were printed from woodblocks: They were engraved on wood; then the background was removed for inking. After the impression but before they were cut out, the leaves were colored by hand or stencil: in the latter case the colors often overlapped. Copper engraving, which was to follow, would allow an important extension of the use of the tarot, which would spread slowly throughout Europe.

France witnessed a recrudescence of interest in the tarot with the appearance in 1781 of the *Monde primitif* of Court de Gibelin, Protestant pastor and Freemason, who claimed that the major arcana were the images from a secret book of ancient Egypt, *The Book of Thoth*.

Much later, in 1856, Eliphas Levi, in his *Dogme et rituel de la haute-magie*, was the first author to establish a parallel between the twenty-two major arcana and the twenty-two letters of the Hebrew alphabet, which led numerous students to occultism and the divinatory tarot.

In 1889, Oswald Wirth, a Swiss occultist and disciple of the Marquis Stanislas de Guaita, published his own set of tarot cards in a limited edition of a book of studies on the subject. The same year saw an erudite work by Gerard Encausse, under the pseudonym of Papus, on the Kabbalistic tarot. In the same period in England, MacGregor Mathers wrote a book on divination by tarot cards. At the same time Mathers and some friends founded the hermetic order of the Golden Dawn, which counted Aleister Crowley among its most distinguished members, along with Arthur Edward Waite and the Irish poet William Butler Yeats. Waite in his turn published *The Pictorial Key to the Tarot*, still used, and Crowley was responsible for the appearance of *The Book of Thoth*, based on the symbolist drawings of Lady Frieda Harris. From England the occultist movement migrated to the United States, where it experienced a great vogue.

In the Anglo-Saxon world new tarots constantly appeared, but most French followers used the Marseilles cards, reissued by Paul Marteau in 1930, when he was in charge of B. P. Grimaud, the well-known manufacturers of playing cards.

The Marseilles tarot, of all those now used, has the easiest symbolism to understand. The cards have not been distorted, like so many others, by the fantasies of their creators and the vibrations of their thought. They are more neutral and their imagery is profoundly moving because it is simpler and more distinct than the others. That is why this deck has been taken as a model for this present work.

Whether it is a question of reprinting old cards or making new designs, it would be tedious here to give an exhaustive list of all the sets of cards that collectors may now obtain. There are more than fifty different decks available.

The Chariot

Standing in a triumphal chariot, the Magician, who had become the male lover in the previous card, has finally chosen his path. He advances, drawn by two horses, one red, meaning action, and the other blue, meaning spirit. The chariot that carries souls in evolution is flesh-colored and represents the intermediate medium between heaven and earth. The soul must not despise the flesh and blood of its embodiment, destined to be subdued and transmuted like a work of alchemy. In many tarot decks, the letters S and M, sign of royalty, are on the front of the chariot. They may also stand for sulphur and mercury, elements of the Great Work.

The driver stands on the diagonal axis of the four columns, signifying the four elements, which he easily controls.

The two women who caused the male lover to hesitate have been replaced by the two moons that the chariot driver wears on his shoulders in memory of the past. At last he has established the duality of body and spirit in perfect equilibrium and reunited opposites. He is calm, serene, sure of himself. He advances triumphantly. His golden crown shows that he reigns over the physical, intellectual, and spiritual worlds; this is confirmed by his scepter.

After the Hierophant's message of peace to mankind, the chariot driver represents the aspect of Christ that said, "I bring not peace but a sword." This symbolizes that struggle in which man confronts himself. His garment is red; therefore, he takes action, but his blue breastplate protects him—spirit rules matter. The chariot wheels advance meanwhile, for they are flesh-colored; later on they will become the Wheels of Fortune.

Traditionally the chariot is associated with the Sun in its heavenly orbit; it is Apollo's chariot when he is identified as the sun god. It is also Ezekiel's chariot, the *Merkabah*, often referred to by the Kabbalists. In all the ancient religions there is a heavenly chariot that rolls over all obstacles. The team of horses symbolizes the senses, the needs, and passions of man, his physical nature. The driver is the spiritual nature of man. Closer to our time, fairy stories have turned this chariot symbol into a coach.

In Zen Buddhism, Buddha's vehicle is a chariot drawn by a white ox. In ancient China, the chariot was the means of demonstrating the skill and virtue of princes and their ability to rule. In the *Rig Veda*, the chariot master is Agni, or Prana, the breath that enlivens. It is the Logos, the Word, the first creator, which pervades the universe. Vedic tradition made it the soul's medium for the duration of an incarnation.

The advancing chariot forces the Lover to emerge from reflection to see what is around him and to guide his progress to the highest summits. It is the grasp of man's knowledge that little by little discloses the meaning of things and reaches out to others to understand them and identify with them.

This is a card of triumph, of success and good health. It is personal action in space and time. It indicates favorable travels, whether in actuality or in spirit or feeling. It stands for intelligent evolution, perseverance, escape, success, and progress, advancement, diplomacy. It is the happy result of physical and spiritual forces being in balance.

Badly placed, this card may indicate disaster, an accident, a risk of blinding through headlong haste, rage, arguments, sometimes ambition that seeks world dominance.

The Chariot is associated with the seventh Sephirah, Netzach (triumph, victory) and the letter *zayin* of the Hebrew alphabet: the weapon that brings victory (it is drawn like an arrow).

The Chariot is also part of the constellation of the Great Bear, made up of seven stars. The Romans called them the seven oxen, or *septem triones*, which gave us the word *septentrion*, the north of the terrestrial sphere.

The Chariot bears the number 7, number of the universe made up by 3, the number of heaven, plus 4, the number of earth.

Before Christianity, the number 7 was considered the manifestation of cosmic order. 7 has long been considered a symbol of eternal life, a signifier of death and resurrection.

In the Old and New Testaments, the number 7 is repeated more than 700 times, and Islam often refers to it. The Kabbalah, the Indian philosophy of *Vedanta*, and Paracelsus all speak of the seven levels of man. The ziggurats, the Babylonian temples built to bring earth nearer to heaven, had seven stories. The rainbow, a sign of God's alliance with Noah, has seven colors.

7 is the key number of the material world. In dice, the total of the numbers on opposite faces always gives the number 7.

1

3

2

Passive, receptive, fertile, the Moon symbolizes the night, humidity, the unconscious, the imaginary. It stands for inspiration, intuition, clairvoyance. It is the most feminine of all the signs. 1. The Moon from the Besançon tarot. 2. The Moon of Jacques Vieville, with its spinner, comes out of a tradition nearer to ourselves, that of the playing-card makers of Rouen and Brussels in the middle of the seventeenth century. 3. The Moon of the Visconti-Sforza deck has the bottom of her robe strangely blended with the outline of the mountains. Page 29: A woodblock cut by a card maker (Colmar, eighteenth century). Unterlinden Museum.

Justice

Like the Empress, Justice sits facing forward on her throne. She has changed the shield and scepter for a sword and scales. Good and evil coexist. Both make up equal parts of the world order. The two scales are for measuring the good and the evil. If the two scales are superimposed we get the number 8, symbol of infinity when it is laid down, and the number of this card.

Through the scales Justice works internally to find perfect equilibrium. At this level of knowledge, man undertakes a definite classification. Revolutions are necessary in order to arrive at and maintain a proper balance. The scales call to mind the duality of the world, the equilibrium for which we strive both internally and externally.

Justice needs a sword to enforce her decisions. The sword represents temporal power and aspires to keep the rule of fairness among men. It should always be more dissuasive than punitive.

Justice also wears a blue cloak and has therefore a high level of knowledge; she can also act immediately, thanks to the red color of her dress.

This card has no white or green, and there is little flesh color; here matter is only slightly represented. Only her hair and hands remind us of her understanding of earthly values. Her plaited hair proves to us her desire for unity and the coming together of opposites. She wears a yellow crown on her head, indicating that her power is of divine origin. This crown is placed on a cap, resembling that of a magistrate, on which we see the solar sign indicating self-knowledge.

Justice is seated on a solid and unshakable throne. Moreover, number 8, her number, equals 4 plus 4, and 4, the Emperor's number, stands for stability. Rising from the throne are two gilded columns, joined by a veil of the same color signifying the work of self-examination. These columns recall those of Solomon's temple. When Hiram, the architect of the temple, cast the bronze for those columns, he named the left one *Jachin*, stability and will, and the right one *Boaz*, force but also prudence.

These columns also resemble those that surround the median axle of the Tree of the Sephiroth: The left column is sternness, and that on the right is mercy, the one in the middle being fairness. These columns of the Tree of Life define Justice—sternness of judgment tempered with mercy result in perfect justice.

Justice is man confronting himself, facing the necessity to put order and judgment into his life. Justice coordinates and untangles chaos. Without her, nothing could exist, because order reigns all through the universe. Man may act according to his free will, but the law is above all and interposes itself between his desires and the will of God. Early or late we gather the fruits of our desires.

Here we have the law of cause and effect, the boomerang, the karma of the Hindus, the weighing of souls by Anubis. Inasmuch as we are thinking beings, we are all judges, because to think is to judge. One should never condemn others: He who condemns exercises a right that does not belong to him, for his judgment is based only on his subjective experience. One must be aware of one's own limits when one conveys a judgment; justice must be the highest knowledge.

This card of balance represents harmony, order, integrity, honor, stability, self-control, law, but also harshness, discipline, overconcern with trifles, respect for rank, submission to convention, the inevitable consequence of every action.

Badly placed, it can indicate intolerance, the constraint of law, formalism, and legal troubles including divorce.

It can indicate kidney disease, but also a return to natural equilibrium. It corresponds to the eighth Sephirah, Hod: praise and glory. Justice manifests the glory of God and guarantees man equality in creation. Justice corresponds to the eighth letter of the Hebrew alphabet, *cheth*: the barrier one may not pass in order not to injure others or impinge on their freedom.

This arcanum bears the number 8, sign of infinity and eternity, the first cubic number, which represents the earth not from the outside but in its inner mass. It has been called the number of Pluto. For the Pythagoreans, 8 was the number of justice, prudence, and reflection. The Egyptian god Thoth—Hermes to the Greeks—was designated as lord of the number 8.

The *Kua*, trigrams conceived by the emperor Fu-Hsi after the Chinese tradition and which make up the I Ching (the "Book of Changes"), are eight in number. According to that book, it was under their influence that the world took shape.

Justice has two aspects: the outer, which rules our moral and social life, and the inner, which rules our consciousness, that is to say, man face to face with himself.

A Kabbalistic Science

In heaven to learn is to see; on earth to remember.

Happy the man who has gone through the Mysteries. He knows the beginning and end of life.

—*Pindar*

The most celebrated occultists—Court de Gibelin, Eliphas Levi, Papus, Oswald Wirth, Arthur Waite, Aleister Crowley, MacGregor Mathers, and many others—have related the twenty-two major arcana of the tarot to the twenty-two letters of the Hebrew alphabet. They assume that the order of letters is not random.

Each letter corresponds to a number according to its position, a hieroglyph according to its form, and a symbol in its relationship to the other letters. All derive from the first, *aleph* (the Magician), whose origin is beyond comprehension as it stands for the Uncreated, En Soph of the *Sepher Yezirah* (or *Book of Creation*, the principal source of the Kabbalah). It is the Logos, which is the beginning of all things, their cause and source, the central principle from which everything emanates, the origin of all thought and activity. As revealed in the Gospel of John: "In the beginning was the Word, and the Word was with God and the Word was God." *Aleph* gives rise to *beth*, second letter in the Hebrew alphabet, principle of *bereshit*, which signifies genesis and which begins the story of creation. *Beth* is born from *aleph* as Eve was born from Adam to become the mother of humanity. In the Kabbalah (from the Hebrew *gabbalah*, "tradition") these twenty-two letters are the matrix of the creation. One sees a similar principle at work in the Qur'an, which contains for Muslims all that needs to be said on man, the world, and the universe. For the ancient Chinese, the sixty-four hexagrams of the I Ching, which are derived from eight trigrams, are ultimately reducible to two principals yin and yang, out of whose constant interplay emerge all forms. Similarly the Vedas serve to contain the entire universe.

The Tao is equivalent to the En Soph. It cannot be grasped; it is being and nonbeing. Each gives rise to the other. It is indivisible, undetermined, beyond time and space. Out of it 1 arises, out of 1, 2, and out of 2, 3. Similarly En Soph, the creative principal of the Kabbalah, contains and fills the universe. To bring the world into existence it engenders the ten Sephiroth, its emanations. The Sephiroth can also be seen as descriptive of man's evolution from nonbeing. They reveal the mysteries of creation, demonstrating how multiplicity arises from unity. Each Sephirah emanates from its predecessor. One can compare them to the ten avatars of Vishnu and to Avicenna's Neoplatonist doctrine in which the tenth emanation corresponds to the intelligence that produces all human souls.

The Tree of the Sephiroth

The ten Sephiroth are connected by the twenty-two paths of wisdom. These correspond to the twenty-two cards of the major arcana and represent a synthesis of the totality of experience and knowledge. (See the diagram on page 37.)

The Kabbalah was for many centuries an oral teaching transmitted from one generation of initiates to the next until it was finally set down in the *Zohar* (*Book of Splendors*) by Rabbi Simon Ben Jochai. The *Zohar* is an esoteric commentary on the first five books of the Bible, the Torah.

The Tree of Life of the *Sepher Yezirah* can be considered as a mandala and as such deserving of meditation. From the perspective of the initiate, here macrocosm meets microcosm. By employing symbols he can enter into contact with different spheres of nature.

The first division to be noted in contemplating the Tree of Life is that of the three vertical columns, which are the three paths of prana described in yoga: *ida*, *pingala*, and *sushumna*. The central column can also be regarded as the Tao, which is flanked by yin and yang.

The Hanged Man of the tarot of Charles VI. This highly symbolic figure lets himself be guided by Divine Will. For him solid ground is in the heavens; he has no contact with earth. Thus he is spiritually elevated. This card bears the number 12. "The root of the sphere, the number of perfection; 12 × 12 is perfection multiplied by itself" (Paul Claudel).

The Hermit

In some French packs of the tarot, particularly those of Marseilles, the Hermit is written with an H (normally it would be "Ermite" in French), doubtless referring to Hermes Trismegistus, the master of initiation.

The Hermit has a flesh-colored beard and hair, to emphasize that his destiny is human, but he goes into the desert to commune with himself and probe the depths of his soul, aided by his staff, his lantern, and his cape.

The blue cape of the Hermit, because of its spirituality, regulates the passions let loose by his red gown. This mysterious old man faces toward the right—he acts, but his aim is divine.

Having established order out of chaos, he has retired from life. He advances only after having sounded the earth with his staff to learn where to place his foot to absorb the telluric power. The staff is the symbol of the road he must take here below and the weapon that allows him to defend himself against injustice. It is also the staff entwined by the serpent, beloved by Asclepius, for the Hermit is doctor of the soul as well as the body.

His right sleeve, lined with white, seeks truth through purity, his right hand holds a lantern that lights up the darkness. However, he hides this lantern with his sleeve: His search remains hidden. His light can blind those who are not ready to look at it. The Hermit knows that very few can come near the truth and that it is better to keep his secret knowledge to himself.

Alone, he sees the light of his lantern, which is also the light of his intelligence, his personal illumination. This brightness is not superficial, because the Hermit probes the inside of things while advancing on his inner path.

The slow and solitary progress of this old man allows him to bring peace; faced only with himself, he cannot meet with antagonism around him. He also brings truth, not intellectual truth but absolute certainty buried in the obscurity of his knowledge, which will light up that obscurity as his lantern does the darkness.

The Hermit is one of the stern tarot cards, but he is stern only with himself. He knows that none should judge his fellow creatures and, if he leads us to the next arcanum, the Wheel of Fortune, he will let us be judge of our thoughts and acts, which will animate that wheel in one sense or another.

The Hermit brings us his knowledge, his inner strength, his informed counsel, his experience, his medical knowledge and solicitude, although he humbly avows, like Socrates: "I know that I know nothing." He meditates in his refuge, ripens his thought, and exhorts us to prudence. Sometimes he indicates austerity, chastity, celibacy, old age.

Badly placed, the card foretells loneliness, delay, fear, sadness, misanthropy, poverty, despondency, and also avarice. It indicates, too, the cares of age and often rheumatism.

It corresponds to the ninth Sephirah, Yesod, the Foundation, the Being in power, in Becoming, and the letter *teth* of the Hebrew alphabet, which is the ideogram of a serpent swallowing its own tail, symbol of energy rising. This sign indicates a shield, which means security and protection.

The Hermit bears number 9, which is total passivity. If 9 is added to another number, whatever it is, the theosophical number remains the same ($43 = 4 + 3 = 7$; $439 = 4 + 3 + 9 = 16 = 1 + 6 = 7$). It destroys itself while remaining the same, and is regenerated. It is the sum of numbers: It is the last number in the manifested universe, at the same time the beginning and the end. If the first nine numbers are added up, we get 45, which is $4 + 5 = 9$. It is the complete number of the total analysis, the multiplication leading to unity, the transposition to new planes, the end of a cycle.

For the Greeks, and in particular for Parmenides, 9 expressed the totality of being and related to absolute values. In Homeric writings 9 had a ritual value. The nine Muses were born of Zeus after nine nights of love. 9 is the length of gestation, of fruitful research; it is the culmination of creation.

To the Chinese, 9 is the center and the axis of the earth: *Kien Mu*. The imperial Chinese throne had nine steps, and there are nine Buddhist gods. The *Tao Te Ching* is composed of 81 chapters (9×9). For Avicenna there was only the number 9 or its multiples, or one more, for the numerical signs have only 9 characters and values, including zero. Liturgically, the novena corresponds to completion or achievement. We find the repetition of three times three in many religious rites. According to Denis the Areopagite, the angels are ranged in nine choirs or triads; perfection in perfection, order in order, unity in unity. Is it not strange that the difference between a number and its inverse will always be divisible by 9?

These forms, which render with meticulous care each symbolic detail, permit us, by visualizing their images and uttering their traditional names, to encounter the force that lies behind each of the Sephiroth. The ten Sephiroth correspond to the action of divine forces in each of these spheres. When we understand perfectly the significations of the arcana we see clearly the Sephiroth and their connection.

The Ten Sephiroth: Illumination and Divination

The Tree of Life is infinite in its application, as is the tarot. The union of these two systems points out a way of balancing the conflicting elements in the inner life of man and of bringing them into a state of harmony. The tarot provides a key to understanding the Sephiroth. From one point of view, all divinatory systems, in fact, find their inspiration in the Tree of Life. From another, tarot, astrology, and the Kabbalah are not three separate esoteric systems but three aspects of the same system, each contributing to a fuller understanding of the other.

So we see that the ten Sephiroth are keys to illumination, and the twenty-two paths symbolizing the relations between microcosm and macrocosm are the keys to divination, thanks to a sort of spiritual diagnostic.

The four aces are assigned to Kesser, which represents "I am that I am." Kesser is the origination of the elements—earth, water, fire, and air—represented by coins, cups, staves, and swords.

Kesser corresponds to the skull; it shines with pure white light above Adam Cadmon, universal man. The rabbis called this light *Yechidah*; the Egyptians named it *Sah*; the Hindus, the lotus with a thousand petals. It is the kernel of pure spirit whence emanates multiplicity. To Kesser is assigned Union with God, the ultimate goal of all the mystics: the perfection of the Great Alchemical Work.

The 2s of the minor arcana correspond to Chochmah, the second Sephirah. This Sephirah is energetic, positive, male. Chochmah is a representation of that energy that for the Hindus is embodied in the lingam, for the Greeks in the phallus. It is the tower and the scepter. In its primitive essence, it is dynamic strength, the divine spark, the vital force. It refers to the left side of the face. It brings forth activity in the world.

The 3s are represented by Binah, the third Sephirah and third point on the upper triangle in the Tree of Life. Binah is the feminine principal. Kesser is all-powerful

Woman Reading Cards (Restoration engraving). The psychic images that radiate from the cards provoke a sort of interior illumination that makes it possible to read the future inscribed in present time.

The Wheel of Fortune

The Wheel symbolizes those rhythms that rule us, the world revolving, the eternal new beginning. It is the roundabout of the universe, with good succeeding evil, day after night, death after life, every concept bearing its converse.

The Wheel of Fortune is also identified with the Wheel of Life in Tibetan Buddhism. The Buddhist Wheel of Life has six spokes because there are six classes of beings. It is also the *Rota Mundi* of the Rosicrucians. Only the center of the cosmic wheel is still, but the *Tao* teaches us that it is the empty lane that makes the chariot roll.

The wheel is well known from the imagery of ancient times and the Middle Ages as a symbol of change. For the Greeks and Romans, Fortune was furnished with a wheel. In prehistoric times, when the wheel was yet undiscovered, we find circles resembling solar wheel engraved on neolithic rocks. To C. G. Jung, the rose windows of cathedrals represent man's self transposed to the cosmic plane.

The Zodiac is a wheel, but the word in Greek means "living being." The chakras energy centers of the human body in Indian philosophy, are also represented by wheels. The wheel is a universal solar symbol. It corresponds to the world, with the hub being the still center of it and the circle the manifestation that emanates from it.

In Tibetan Buddhism mandalas are primary tools for meditation. They are often circular. In fact, the shape of the circle comprehends the entire cosmos, the Samsara of estern philosophy and the Kabbalistic *rota*.

The Wheel of Fortune is the card of blind fate, of the lottery, of chance or mischance. It is the arcanum of karma, neither good nor bad, of those endlessly revolving cycles with the same joys and the same ordeals. It is the card of adventurers and explorers, of all those who either cannot or will not stay still.

Badly placed, it foretells blows of Fate, disturbing anxieties, upsets. It always signals a change, for good or evil, according to the present state of health.

This card is linked to the tenth Sephirah, Malchus, the Kingdom, which is the final end of all the activities of the Tree of the Sephiroth, the nadir of the wheel's rotation, the lowest point in the descending arc through which all life must pass before rising again toward its origin.

It is also associated with the letter *yod*, the initial of the secret name of God. For the Kabbalists, it is the starting point of the divine Will, the union of the Creator with his creation.

The Wheel of Fortune bears the number 10, formed by 1, being, and 0, nonbeing, absolute nothingness, which is yet ready to give birth, the universe, illimitable space. For Pythagoras, 10 defined matter. The creative principle of God, the Logos, penetrated negative material space and fertilized it, and 10 was born.

Number 1, the Magician's number, the first manifestation of God, is now joined with the 0 of infinity, which becomes a number when it is preceded by another. 10 is then a new beginning on a higher plane. It is no longer 1, an individual being, but is now a part of the All. It was the most sacred number for Pythagoreans, the symbol of universal creation on which they took an oath. They said of the *tetrakis*—the sum of the first four numbers—that everything emanates from it and returns to it, so that it is the image of the totality of the moving world and of the return to unity.

When we contemplate the Wheel of Fortune, we must think of a change originating from decisions outside ourselves, that is, from chance, which makes things good or bad from our point of view and which is not necessarily for the best.

Omar Khayyam extolled this image thus: "This wheel on which we turn is like a magic lantern. The sun is the lamp, the world is the screen. We are passing images."

The Wheel of Fortune depicts a flesh-colored wheel, the Wheel of Life, which has six blue-and-white spokes moved by divine forces. It augurs harmony because 6 is a perfect number standing for the union of the human soul with the divine spirit. But this Wheel of Fate rotates in matter. The handle is white and therefore pure, but no one appears to turn it. Its perpetual rotation cannot be stopped.

On this Wheel of Becoming, we see three animals, half-monkey, half-monster. The one on the left, dominated by his instincts and senses, descends into matter, doubtless against his will; his energy is from his animal nature. The second animal, on the right of the wheel, is conscious and intelligent, for he is yellow; he looks heavenward as he climbs up. The third, seated on top of the wheel, is man crowned, spiritual man, for he is colored blue, his wings allow him to rise, and his sword of justice is white and pure.

Strength

It might seem surprising to see Strength represented by a pretty young woman of frail appearance. This is the power of the feminine, compounded of sweetness and patience. It is internal power, moral strength and courage. Strength easily overcomes the natural brute force of the lion, for she subjugates by will alone, using the power of the unconscious.

This young woman wears as a hat the lazy eight, the sign of infinity, which recalls that of the Magician. She is also aware of eternity, and over her gown glowing with internal blue light falls a red cape that lights up her power of life and love.

Her yellow sleeves direct the energy of love, which flows into her flesh-colored hands before overcoming the king of animals. Effortlessly she holds his mouth wide open, for her soul is love, capable of conquering all: spirit is victorious over matter. She is a virgin, not a colossus and embodies spiritual strength, symbol of moral purity.

She recalls the myth of Amphion, son of Jupiter and Antiope, one of the Argonauts, who built the walls of Thebes by the sound of his lyre. Charmed by his melodies, the stones came of their own will and placed themselves one upon another. Boileau wrote in *Poetic Art*, "The stones moved to the chords of Amphion and raised themselves in order on the Theban walls, the birth of harmony producing these miracles."

This card has no background, it represents pure strength operating instinctively. It has no earthly base—everything reaches upward by means of psychic will.

Love is the most powerful force in the world; through it Strength has subdued the lion but has not killed it. Gilgamesh, the hero of the Assyrian epic, did not choke the lion; he stunned it. As an initiate he did not despise his enemies, for the powers of evil excite action; it was enough for him to transform them into beneficial energy and ennoble them by the transmutation.

The virgin of Strength stands on the eleventh plane of knowledge; she knows it is not necessary to kill one's enemies in order to neutralize them, for that would be a waste of energy. One must try to make allies of them by using that energy that flows from the arcanum, and make the power of love shine through the world. Strength is unarmed; she employs only her arms and her power of nonviolence. It is striking, noted C.G. Jung, that the legendary heroes who fought lions were always unarmed. That is because these heroes symbolize the battle against the earthly self; having overcome it, they, like Strength, are One with all life on earth.

The lion is likened to primitive energies—strength, courage, might. He is majestic, noble, king. The *Bhagavad Gita* says that Krishna is the lion among animals. Buddha is considered the lion of Shakya, Christ the lion of Judah. The lion therefore is the destroyer of evil and of ignorance, the symbol of the sun. His astrological sign is situated in August, the hottest month of the year. The lion represents Justice when he is beside the throne of Solomon or those of the kings of France or of medieval bishops.

Strength, then, is active and positive. She takes the violence of instinct and channels it for good. She is the triumph of intelligence over brutality. She is reason and love, which unite to subdue instinct. She is the incarnation of moral and physical health. She is confidence, conquest, bravery, and ambition.

Sometimes she means too much activity, an interference in other people's affairs; also pride, struggle, rashness, competition, anger, and impatience. Badly placed, she may go as far as boasting, outbursts of passion, fury, and despotism.

On the level of health, she indicates tremendous energy, and she represents the heart and cardiac illness.

Strength bears the number 11; she is at the same time the Empress, 3, who has passive intelligence, and Justice, 8, who personifies harmony and equilibrium

After the fullness of 10, a perfect cycle in itself, 11 is the number of excess. It indicates conflict by its ambivalence. It can be the beginning of a renewal of truly the breaking of 10.

11 is imbalance, hypertrophy, and therefore disorder. It is individual initiative that takes no account of cosmic order. Its theosophical addition makes 2, again duality, conflict, internal struggle.

11 brings us back to the pentagram, 5, and the hexagram, 6—that is, to the two stars of microcosm and macrocosm. It is the reunion of these two stars that Strength will achieve after her struggle and her victory. 11 is the chief number for all initiation, especially in its multiples of 22, 33, and 77.

This arcanum suggests to us the intelligent use of strength, wisdom that overcomes by gentleness, the total mastery of self and of others, a brilliant victory.

being but being beyond action. Action emanates from it descending through Chochmah, which cannot be dissociated from its emanation Binah, the Great Mother, archetypical mistress who gives birth to all life. Binah corresponds to the right side of the face. She is the root of materiality, the primordial influence whence arise all forms. Chochmah and Binah are the first set of opposites out of which are established the two flanking columns of the *Sepher Yezirah*. These two fundamental Sephiroth are called Father and Mother. They are virility and femininity, whose creative union calls forth the world. The rabbis who studied the Tree of Life asserted that each Sephirah is negative in relation to the one that precedes it and positive in relation to the one it precedes. This thought can easily be transposed into the microcosm and describes our relationship with those above and below us.

The maternal aspect of Binah appears in the name of *Marah*, the sea, which is given to it. Venus was born from the sea foam and the Virgin Mary is named *Stella Maris*, star of the sea. Binah then completes the superior triad of the *Sepher Yezirah* and is associated with the feminine principle.

Between the three higher Sephiroth and the six that succeed them, there lies a vast gulf that Kabbalists call the Abyss. The first Sephirah on the other side of this gulf is Chesed, Kindness, to which the 4s of the minor arcana and the left arm in the human body correspond. Chesed is the sphere of the archetype of the benevolent ruler, father of his people. It is the first manifest Sephirah. It contains within itself all power, and from it emanate all spiritual virtues.

One cannot separate Chesed from Gevurah, Strength, the number 5, which succeeds it. Gevurah corresponds to the right arm. This is the dynamic Sephirah that drives us onward and overcomes all obstacles. It has the virtues as well as the vices of Mars: energy, courage, but also cruelty and destructiveness. It is the most dynamic and violent of the Sephiroth, the most disciplined as well. It engages in combat but without fury. It spares the injured and oppressed. It inspires fear but also respect. It has an equal and complementary role to Chesed in maintaining equilibrium.

Tiphares, Beauty, is the sixth Sephirah. It is situated in the center of the middle column of the Tree of Life. It is linked to the number 6 and to the chest in the human body. It is the point of equilibrium on the tree. The central column is particularly concerned with consciousness. Tiphares represents the crystallization of the archetypes. In it incarnation takes form. God the Father manifests itself in Kesser, God the Son, the Redeemer, in Tiphares, which is the sphere of the sun, symbol of the energy that this Sephirah radiates. The beauty referred to here is perfect harmony, balance between macrocosm and microcosm. The trunk of the body, to which it corresponds, contains the solar plexus as well as the heart and lungs; these organs govern the circulation and the process of respiration, the signs of life, which maintain the individual's constant interchange of energies with the cosmos. The sixth Sephirah, in its numerological aspect, refers to the cross, leading us to the major arcana: the Lovers, or the crossroads. It is also related to the 6 in the minor arcana, which always implies the idea of choice, hesitation, also victory in battle.

The ten Sephiroth can be schematized according to the vertical columns as well as to three horizontal divisions. The upper triangle represents the fundamental principles of action and passivity, which bring forth manifestation. The central triangle represents this manifestation in its diversity of form and expression.

The four lower Sephiroth belong to the plane of power and form. Here is the incarnation of the limited self, the four elements, matter, mentation, the personality and its powers.

Netzach, Force, is the seventh Sephirah, associated with the 7s in the minor arcana and the loins and legs. Netzach manifests itself in the world of instincts, emotions, and natural forces. It is the domain of Venus and is situated on the column of mercy. In Netzach the mind of man conceives of images that are realized through its emanation, Hod. Netzach is the artist who creates in relationship to Hod, which is more intellectual. The two are indissociable.

Hod, Splendor, is assigned to the number 8 and, like Netzach, corresponds to the loins and the legs. It is also the sphere of Mercury, hence intellect. Here is magic, because Hod brings forth the forms conceived in Netzach. It is in this Sephirah that rational intelligence reveals itself to human consciousness; nature animates living beings. Veiled by Hod, the initiate discerns the Creator hidden behind his creation and aspires to assist the Great Architect of the Universe.

With the 9s of the minor arcana we arrive at Yesod, the Foundation, which is on the column of equilibrium. Yesod corresponds to the organs of reproduction. The text of the *Sepher Yezirah* tells us that the ninth Sephirah justifies the Emanations, purifies and corrects them, that it is the "Vision of the Universal Mechanism." Yesod participates simultaneously in the worlds of matter and spirit. It is the receptacle of the emanations from the other Sephiroth, which it then transmits to Malchus, the physical plane. Yesod is the reflection of the terrestrial plane, the unconscious, the house of Maya, illu-

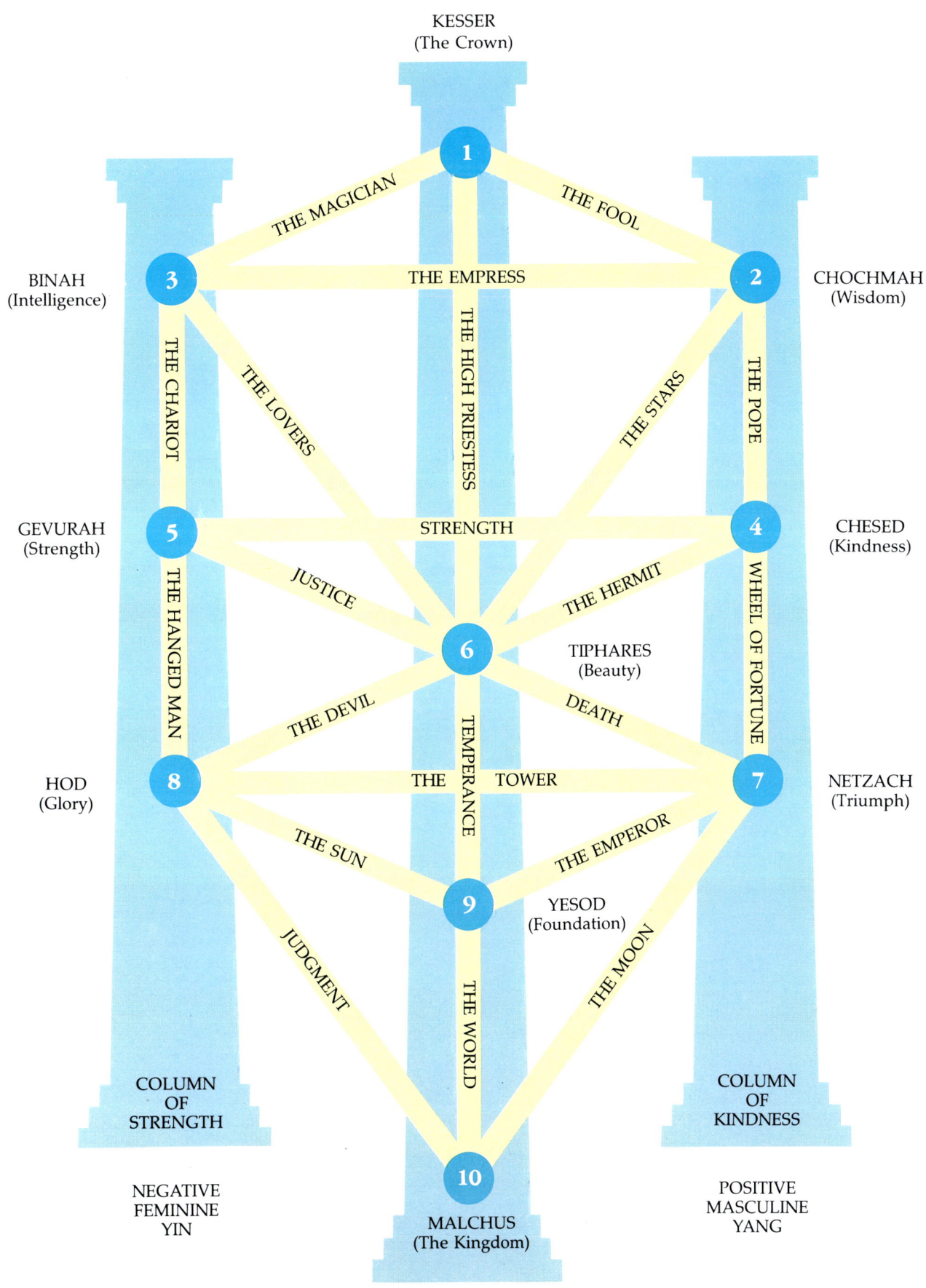

37

1. Temperance of the Visconti-Sforza tarot. This card announces the passage from a lower to a higher state, just as water, the source of life, is purified by circulation. 2. The Wheel of Fortune (Besançon deck). Here great ones are made and unmade. 3. Justice (Besançon deck) reminds us of the laws of balance and karma. 4. With the Devil (Vieville tarot) we enter the world of sex and the passions.

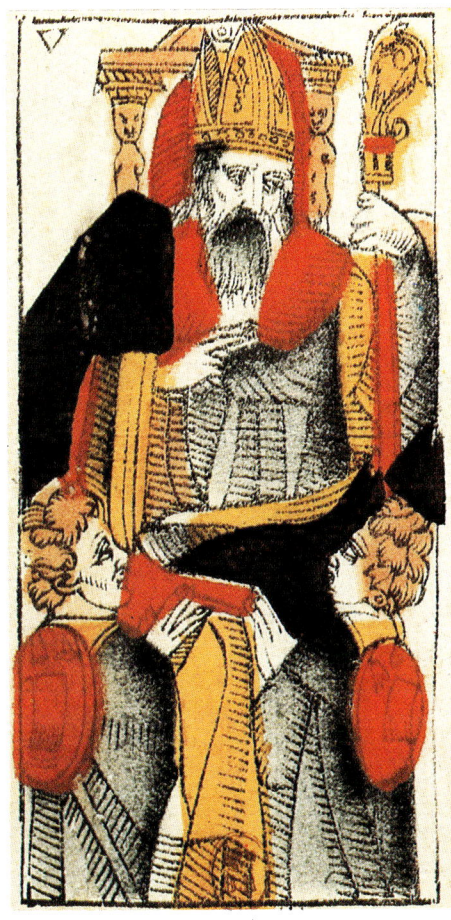

1

2

3

1. The Hierophant of the Vieville tarot wears the bishop's miter, not the three-tiered papal tiara in which he is depicted in most other decks. The Hierophant represents conciliation, the reunion of the celestial and the terrestrial. He bears the number 5, which holds the central position in the first nine numbers and joins them all together. 2. The Lovers (Besançon tarot). How long will he hesitate there at the crossroads of Vice and Virtue, while Cupid draws back his bow? 3. The Magician (Visconti-Sforza deck). This is the first card of the major arcana. He is known by many names: Bateleur, Jongleur, Juggler, Minstrel.... Whatever his name, he invites us to enter upon the game of life.

The Hanged Man

The Hanged Man sacrifices himself for others in complete self-abnegation. His sacrifice is voluntary and in no way resembles torture. He has the relaxed, smiling face of the Magician, but he is suspended by one blue (spiritual) foot, and his legs, sheathed in red (therefore active), are crossed like those of the Emperor but in reverse, a sign of renunciation, that he may reach his development and perfect his inner knowledge. With his foot he makes a cross, an act of will. The cross is one of the four basic symbols: It represents the earth in its dynamic aspect. At its center lies the point of communication between heaven and earth; it is the symbol of the ascension of Christ, savior of the world.

The Hanged Man has no contact with the earth: He has voluntarily withdrawn from its denser influences, material reality escapes him, and he lives in a dream, in another world. He is passive and powerless on the material plane, but his spiritual power is immense. His head, pointing earthward, indicates that he is concerned with earth but only on the spiritual level, for his hair and his feet are blue, and he devotes himself exclusively to the well-being of others.

In the preceding card, Strength, universal love has been realized, and now the Hanged Man sacrifices himself for that love. He has no longer any individual will—his foot and his wrists are bound—and he allows himself to be directed by the divine Will, for his spiritual level is very high. That is why he is upside-down: For him solid ground is above, symbolized by the green of Nature, and not below, because he has no contact at all with the earth.

His soul is suspended between heaven and earth in a state of perfect solitude. The rope always represents the means, as well as the desire, to ascend, as that of the shaman is used to climb the ladder of heaven. It is knotted, suggesting hiddden, magic virtues. It is white, perhaps meaning the silver cord that binds man's spirit to the universal essence; it is the way of concentration by meditation.

The yellow trees, the color of light, unite heaven and earth, or earth and heaven, because the inversion of values in this card in comparison to others reminds us of the *Emerald Tablet*, which appeared in the Middle Ages and was attributed to Hermes Trismegistus: It teaches us that "that which is low is like that which is high and that which is high is like that which is low; from these things are made the miracles of the one thing." The two trees are the columns of the Temple, indicating the spiritual aspirations of the Hanged Man and foretelling the staves of the minor arcana.

The twelve scars on the trees stand for the twelve zodiacal signs. The twelve branches are cut off because the Hanged Man is beyond their action and influence, but their essence is in him. He has absorbed their sap, which is why they have been cut off as useless.

The nine buttons on his spiritually blue jacket remind us of the Hermit. Like him, the Hanged Man seeks truth, but he has chosen a more difficult path to inner knowledge. His sacrifice is that of Christ and the martyrs, who accepted suffering in the hope of giving mankind a better future.

In India, the yogis stand on one leg for days, with a view to reaching perfect control and oblivion of self, together with a higher level of knowledge.

The Hanged Man profits from his lack of action by finding knowledge. His sacrifice is redemptive. He is a mystic, an enlightened prophet, a priest, a patriot.

His self-abnegation brings him clairvoyance, intuition, inspiration, regeneration, telepathy, but on the material plane his life is suspended, blocked off, and pleasure is rare.

Close to other cards that reinforce its tendencies, this card indicates the lack of practicality, a certain utopianism, an extreme sensitivity that can be unhealthy, love that is not returned, apathy, masochism, failure, sometimes drugs.

In the region of health, it can indicate paralysis; it represents the feet and bad circulation.

The Hanged Man bears the number 12, which can be divided by half the digits of its own number, which is very exceptional. Its value was recognized back in the earliest times by Egypt, Chaldea, China, central Asia, Greece, Mexico, Chile, and many African peoples.

12 belongs to the celestial world, and heaven is divided into the twelve zodiacal signs. The year has four seasons of three months; days and nights both have twelve hours. The duodecimal system preceded the decimal, and the lunar cycle of twelve periods has guided man from earliest antiquity.

12 bequeaths to us its aspects of sacrifice, of obstruction, but also of inspiration and development. However, we cannot expect much material satisfaction from it.

Death
(The Arcanum with No Name)

"The thirteenth reappears . . . It is still the first; and it is always the only one."
—Nerval

The thirteenth arcanum of the tarot is sometimes called Death, but very often, especially in the Marseilles cards, it has no name. The act of naming a thing confers power over it. It is for that reason that initiates may be given a secret name, freeing them from the grip of the everyday world. What is nameless is unthinkable; we cannot evoke it or speak of it. A name gives an individualization to what is potential. Death the Destroyer has no name because it opposes the Creative Word.

This anonymous one is also explained by the fact that Death represented by this card is not real death. It is better not to distract the Counselor by this formidable word: This Arcanum is already frightening enough because of the skeleton, the scythe, and the number 13, which is imbued with an evil reputation. In fact, this card is far from being as bad an augury as it appears.

The skeleton is clothed in human flesh and can feel; fatality is therefore less cruel than it was thought to be. Its only aim is to remind us that man's spirit is born from matter and must return to it before being reborn and made sublime. But Death in the tarot is generally only an initiating death, the voluntary death required of Freemasons at the door of the temple before their rebirth, and of all neophytes initiated into the hermetic philosophies. That is confirmed by the black earth strewn with bones, feet, hands, and even heads. This black is the black produced in alchemy as the beginning of the transmutation of metals. Black also represents oblivion, which is the night of the unconscious. Oblivion, sleep, and death are three manifestations of the same principle, maintained at different degrees with differing intensity. In effect, oblivion is to sleep as sleep is to death. We forget: we remember; we sleep: we awaken; we die: we are reborn. We return through the cycles of the Wheel of Fortune. The process of forgetting begins as soon as we die, but the recollection of this memory begins as soon as we are born. This oblivion or forgetfulness has been taught and experimented with in certain yogic practices, also in Kabbalistic teachings and among the Sufis.

In this card, the yellow scythe with a red blade symbolizes the deliberate action that cuts the bonds between the self and the physical body, gathering in life's harvest. The scythe moves from left to right, not from right to left in the traditional movement of the scyther. This inversion means that the scythe does not cut the bonds of life, it preserves them, while cutting away the vicissitudes of evil. It operates within matter.

Standing, his right foot buried in the earth, the skeleton has cut off his left foot, which he was using as a root. Each step forward implies the loss of a little earth. This cut foot symbolizes freedom, death having been cut from his earthly bonds, his past, to become more independent, but the blue and yellow grass allows a glimpse of rebirth in the spiritual world.

The alchemists liken volatile substances, released from matter, to a man with a foot cut off. The decapitated heads are smiling as if they were still living but delivered from the constraints of earthly life.

Death in this card does not mean someone's decease, at least as long as it is not very badly placed, but rather a change, the end of a way of life, the beginning of a new cycle, an alteration not necessarily pleasant but followed by renewal. It means an initiation, a transition, a liberation, a transformation, the victory of the spirit.

It also stands for indifference, asceticism, inflexibility and sometimes fatality, the influence and protection of the dead, old age, sadness, grief, devastation in the material world, and the destruction of projects or enterprises. It is not initiation in itself, but rather the conditions out of which initiation arises.

It stands for osteopathy, everything that concerns the skeleton and bones, and the icy cold of winter.

The sphere contains thirteen spheres whose diameters are a third of its own; the thirteenth sphere, situated at the center, hidden by the other 12, is invisible from the outside, so one may believe it to be nonexistent or dead.

13 corresponds to a dynamic system, but not a universal one, for the activity of the 3 is exercised on the unity of the 10, which contains it and therefore necessarily limits it. It is the key of a partial and relative harmony, whose power is regenerative.

This Arcanum suggests to us a transformation, a change of level, the inexorable march of evolution, the end of a cycle, but it is concerned with material existence, not with the worlds of God and the spirit.

41

Temperance

In the Marseilles tarot cards, [La] Tempérance is not preceded by a definite article, perhaps in order to emphasize all the more the universality of this arcanum to which no limits are set.

Temperance is a winged female, like the Empress, analogous to the queen of heaven, but she has no crown. Therefore she has no spiritual or temporal power except that of pouring a white liquid, perhaps water, the source and origin of life, from a blue (spiritual) chalice into a red one, so that it may be transformed.

The Magician has traveled along a road strewn with ambushes, through the whole world before reaching this new series of major cards. After the arcanum of the black in the great alchemical work, Temperance begins the white by the transformation of water, which purifies matter. After the initiation of the preceding card, we now have continuity, regeneration brought by this angel whose wings are flesh-colored and can raise her up toward the Divine. Temperance does not create, but she transfuses, thanks to the dynamism of her red sleeves and dress, always covered by the blue of spirituality, which is also the color of her hair. She foretells the transition from a lower to a higher state. Man is still struggling in the constraints of matter, but he is beginning to detach himself to reach a more shining destiny.

The yellow earth and the yellow belt and scarf around her neck attest to the solar character of this arcanum, identified with Aquarius, continuity in renewal, man alone face to face with himself and God, finding spiritual freedom after many ordeals.

Water represents Creation emerging from the thought of the Creator. "Everything was water" say the Hindu writings. Genesis evokes the spirit that moved upon the surface of the waters, which was the beginning of creation from En Soph, the emerging point of the Nonmanifest primordial of the Kabbalah. This idea of primordial water is found in the oldest and most diverse traditions. In the Qur'an, God caused pure water to fall from heaven, which would give life to the earth after its death. In the Gospel according to John, Jesus says to a woman of Samaria: "Whosoever drinketh of the water that I shall give him shall never thirst; but the water that I shall give him shall be in him a well of water springing up into everlasting life."

Water effaces all traces of defilement as the baptismal water washes away sin. It is the means of purification used by Muslims before their ritual prayers. Water represents the course of life. Heraclitus of Ephesus said that one never steps into the same river twice because "all is flux, nothing is stationary." Sensations themselves are always different from what they have been. Nothing is reproduced in an exactly identical manner.

Water flowing from one pitcher to another evokes the snake, bound to the telluric powers, to the night of beginning, to the inner psyche, to the libido. It is the kundalini of the Hindus, representing the renewed manifestation of life, or the serpent associated with Vishnu and Shiva, cyclical creation and destruction—life, which is born from death, and death, which ends life. The snake personifies the eternal self-impregnator, the Ouroboros, the snake swallowing its own tail, which also possesses the dynamic of the circle whose movement is infinite.

The chalices Temperance holds evoke the womb in which new life takes shape, and a new cycle begins.

In medieval literature, the chalice was assimilated into the symbolism of the grail, the object of a quest that only a knight as pure as Galahad could hope to reach. It was unattainable for those lacking the necessary degree of inner perfection. It stands for the quest for the absolute and the fullness of humanity in evolution.

This card urges meditation on universal life, harmony, the purification of matter. It corresponds to the search for equilibrium, patience, moderation, serenity, communication, exchange.

Badly placed, it can indicate instability, laziness, apathy, fickleness, prodigality, lack of constraint.

It represents a healer, a practitioner of acupuncture, the circulation of energy and of the blood, the arteries, the white corpuscles, the spleen, and the nervous system.

Temperance bears the number 14. In Egyptian cosmology, the region where the souls of the dead were given up was divided into fourteen parts.

In the Gospel according to Matthew we read: "So all the generations from Abraham to David are fourteen generations; and from David until the carrying away into Babylon are fourteen generations; and from the carrying away into Babylon unto Christ are fourteen generations." 14 equals twice 7, the sacred number whose importance was noted in our discussion of the Chariot.

sion. It is symbolized by the moon and the moon goddess Diana.

The tenth Sephirah, which corresponds to the 10s in the minor arcana, is Malchus, the Kingdom. It is at the base of the Tree of Life on the central column. It corresponds to the anus and the feet. It is isolated; yet it receives the emanations of all the other Sephiroth. It represents the final result of all the activities of the Tree, the nadir of evolution to which all life must arrive before remounting toward the source. Malchus is the sphere of the earth but also its soul. It is the permanent vehicle of manifestation, animated by the forces that flow from Yesod. It is the material functioning of Malchus that makes definable and tangible the energies of the higher planes. The emanations of the other Sephiroth are themselves illuminated as soon as they find a form and are reflected in the material aspect of Malchus.

We who are incarnated in physical bodies inhabit the world of Malchus, but by treading the path of the initiates we have the possibility of returning to Kesser. Thus One becomes Many and Many can return to be reabsorbed into the One.

The ten Sephiroth and the twenty-two pathways that connect them form a mystical system that describes the human soul's relationship with the cosmos. These twenty-two pathways, which link the macrocosm with the microcosm, are the keys to divination. They allow us to make a very precise diagnosis of a spiritual condition, Since what happens to us is the result of our own actions, a diagnosis of our spiritual state will reveal future events before they actually occur.

Through an arduous but enriching training based on visualization and concentration, the study and contemplation of the Tree of Life, as well as of the major arcana of the tarot, will develop certain mental powers.

The Face Cards in the Tarot and the Hebrew Alphabet

Many of the esoterists who have studied the tarot have correlated the four sets of face cards in the tarot with the four letters in the sacred name of God in Hebrew, Yahweh, which is written YHWH. In this schema the kings are correlated to the letter *yod*, which signifies the hand. It is the hand of the Cosmic Artist that provides creation with its élan vital. It is this hand that Job invokes in the words "Your hands formed me. . . . You have fashioned me as clay." *Yod* is the encounter of the Creator with his creation. *Yod* is the first letter in the name of God and presides over the energy that this letter unleashes.

The queens receive, increase, and transmit the primordial energy of the kings. They correspond to the letter *he* in which is symbolized life as breath. In the *Zohar* the *he* came to present itself before the En Soph and was given as its function to constitute with *yod* and *vav* the sacred name. The letter *he* is the symbol of life in its origins. When man emerges from the clay shaped by the *yod*, the *he* breathes life into him.

The queens represent the second stage of creation, which is completed when all four letters are brought together.

The knights represent the power of *vav*, which means "hook." The letter *vav* acts as a conjunction in Hebrew writing; it serves a coordinating function. It unites the two *he*'s between which it lies and joins them to *yod*. It animates the reunited energies of the kings and queens. It is the manifestation of their union and its intellectual image.

With the pages we arrive at *he* again, the last letter in the name of God. This *he* represents the final stage of the original energy which, launched into manifestation, is crystallized in materiality but loses itself in the silence of the Uncreated.

It would seem difficult to comprehend these relationships without possessing a profound knowledge of the Kabbalah, and it would be as pretentious as it is ridiculous to suppose that we could explain in a few words what Kabbalists devote lifetimes to studying. Moreover, there are as many interpretations of the Kabbalah as there are Kabbalists, which doesn't make the approach to this tradition any easier. It is, however, extremely interesting to survey the broad lines of thought in this tradition, which is so often referred to in studying the tarot.

Let us also note the ubiquity of the number 22. In addition to the twenty-two major arcana, pathways between the Sephiroth and letters of the Hebrew alphabet, there are twenty-two letters in most ancient alphabets: Phoenician, Chaldean, Sabean, Coptic, Ethiopian, Egyptian. There are also twenty-two books in the Old Testament and twenty-two chapters in the book of Revelations. The books that comprise the Zend Avesta have twenty-two chapters . . .

(*Following pages*) Cheater with Ace of Diamonds, by Georges de la Tour (*Musée du Louvre*). This cardplayer cannot be acquainted with the teaching of the tarot. Trickery is useless. Sooner or later man is confronted with himself and with the truth.

The Devil

With the Devil, we enter the world of the flesh, passions, and sex. The Devil resembles a man but he has a woman's breasts—perhaps he is a hermaphrodite? His body is flesh-colored and therefore made of matter, but his blue legs and wings recall the original divine state of this fallen angel. His wings resemble those of a bat more than of an angel. He has become Lucifer, without his own reality and existing only through man, whose primitive instincts he has corrupted. Only man can engender a spirit that is identified with the matter from which the Prince of Darkness draws his energy.

His yellow helmet, from which sprout horns of the same color, denotes an original intelligence. The white sword without a hilt, and therefore difficult and dangerous to hold, is in touch with the divine world, but this contact remains material, the Devil's desire for action being limited by the matter on which his feet rest.

Two imps, perhaps fauns, enslaved by the flesh, recall the kneeling neophytes before the Hierophant. Like them, these two personages are reduced in size in order to make plain the importance of the demon who has already tempted the Lovers. One appears to be a man, the other a woman. Both, completely naked and flesh-colored, have ears and horns like animals suggesting the bestial origins of man, while their long tails link them to the earth. They are chained together and therefore slaves to their carnal passions. They represent the positive and negative power of instinct. If we sublimate our passions, we can transform sexual energy into the creative force, thus conquering Satan with his own weapons.

This sexuality, however, is not to be despised, for it is the only way to transmit earthly life. His sexual life helps man to maintain his equilibrium and gives him an ideal that allows him to exercise his sense of sacrifice, to renounce egotism, and to dedicate himself to another, to the nonself. The legend of Tristan and Isolde is a perfect example.

The Devil is bisexual because Adam, symbol of the first form of humanity, was bisexual: God created Eve out of his body. The two sexes seek one another in their earthly life and are united for only a short moment in the sexual act in order to procreate. Bisexuality is always present in man, who bears within him the inclinations of both sexes in various degrees of development.

This demon is not as black as is often thought. We all carry the generative force within us, but we do not know how to use it and are content to remain its slaves.

For the Cathars, Satan was the Demiurge, a creator of the created world, because since God could not be perceived or comprehended, he could represent only the uncreated, only spirit.

The Devil is also the Baphomet worshipped by the Templars and the god Pan, whose Greek name means "all."

We should not allow the dark powers of the Devil to weaken our knowledge, for that means the fall of the spirit in an irresistible desire to gratify one's passions at any price.

The Devil warns of the perils facing men who wish to rule. He is the ladder of temptation in contrast to that of spiritual advancement. He represents that excess that led a religion of love to light the fires of the Inquisition. He is pure instinct without reason, but he draws great material activity from his vitality. He is both good and evil. He rules through the fascination released by his magnetism. His occult powers are animal but compelling.

This card is neither good nor bad in itself. Like magic, it is a double-edged weapon. It may indicate the most resounding success or the most profound failure.

Badly placed, it signals treachery, meanness, unscrupulousness, deceit, greed, intrigue, cheating in affairs of money. It indicates witchcraft and casting of spells, therefore excess in one's love life, passion, base instincts, lust, and perversion.

It evokes poison, overindulgence, insomnia, a demanding and dangerous sexuality, magnetism as a healing means.

Everyone can chase the Devil from his life. In the psalms, David proclaims: "Let God arise, let his enemies be scattered; let them also that hate him flee before him. As smoke is driven away, so drive them away: as wax melteth before the fire, so let the wicked perish at the presence of God."

15 is a number divisible by 3, the divine number, and by 5, the number of Christ and man. It is the sum of the first five numbers.

The Devil must appear to us as a warning. As Goethe says, "Only he who rules himself can free himself from the power which enslaves all others."

The Devil rules over power and social success, the use of force, money, and sex.

The Tower

The Prince of Aquitaine at the stricken tower . . .
—Nerval, *The Unfortunate One*

The Tower has had its top struck by a lightning bolt. In some decks it is called the House of God, and sometimes the Tower Struck by Lightning. A flesh-colored edifice, it symbolizes earthly ambition. It personifies the human desire to draw near to the divine power. It is a ladder that allows man to climb toward the cosmos; but the Tower is not the Tree of Life, which rears up to heaven; it is only the work of men puffed up with pride, already manifested by the Devil, who wishes to raise himself up to the level of God by material means.

Man, knowing himself to be the king of creation, wants to meet with the king of heaven. This is the mythical subject of the Tantalus story. It is also the biblical Tower of Babel, destroyed like the temple by the hand of God.

Here the lightning represents divine justice. God punishes man for trying to make himself divine. Pride prevents man from rising above the human state.

The lightning bolt, the attribute of Zeus and of the Vedic god Indra, is a manifestation of God's wrath. It introduces the idea of divine power, just and infinite but beneficial, for his power is always generative. This image of the lightning bolt is not frightening in this arcanum; it is not a vivid light, but only plumes of red and yellow, and therefore intelligent and active; they sweep the top of the tower like tongues of purifying fire. This destruction allows us to distinguish the useful from the useless and to build the promise of a better life from the ruins; it is a process that recalls the ambivalent action of Shiva, Hindu god of both destruction and creation.

The Tower, the first building in the major arcana, is surmounted by four battlements, the number of matter. Only the top of the Tower has been struck, because it has reached an excessive height. Three blue windows decorate the façade; the two smaller ones are eyes open on the spiritual plane; the middle window might be considered the chakra of the third eye, Ajna, which binds man to the spiritual. These three points have escaped pride and are untouched by the lightning.

Two men are falling to the ground from the top of the Tower but are apparently unhurt. Their hair, feet, and arms are blue, and therefore it is spirit that is alluded to and not matter as in the preceding card. In The Devil, matter, blinds man; in the Tower, it is ambition that prevents him from finding the true balance between spirit and matter. This ambition urges him to raise himself too high, forgetting that high roofs attract lightning.

The blue, white, and red drops that fall from the sky represent the positive energy engendered by this destruction, and the tufts of green grass and the two white stones are the promise of a new edifice, one better adapted to reach heaven.

The athanor, the furnace of the alchemists, was in the form of a tower to show us that transmutations are in a sense a rising up. The alchemical texts teach us that "when the son has become strong enough, he must break the chalice as the chick breaks the eggshell that holds him."

We should not be too disturbed at the sight of this card, although it is nevertheless a stern warning. Like the scorpion with which it is compared, it shows destruction before reconstruction—it is autumn, the period during which Nature sleeps, giving the impression that she is dead, before awakening to a new cycle.

Psychic mistakes can be overcome. Sometimes preconceived ideas must be wiped out to make a tabula rasa. Fatality, catastrophe, wounded pride, rigid dogmatism, all lead to a downfall; material vexations always have psychic repercussions, often agonizing but sometimes constructive.

This card foretells an operation, an act of surgery, sometimes an accident if it is associated with cards announcing displacement, or it may be nervous depression or a miscarriage.

Generally it means undertaking thoughtless risks, a merited punishment, ambition chastised for being overweening, or simply great rage, a divorce, a failure, anxiety whether justified or not.

16 equals 4 x 4, that is to say, matter multiplied by matter. Supermatter calls for destruction. $1 + 6 = 7$, the key number of the material world. It is curious to ascertain that it was the October 16, 1307, when Guillaume de Nogaret ordered the imprisonment of the Templars accused of having worshiped Baphomet; that was the end of the Temple. As for Saint Augustine, in the twenty-two books that comprise *The City of God*, he dedicated the third book to death, the sixteenth to the destruction of Sodom by the fire of heaven, and the twentieth to the Resurrection.

The Star

The Star, sometimes called the Stars, represents Temperance with having nothing more to hide. Her nakedness is a sign of humility. Naked as Eve in her original purity, naked as truth emerging from the well, see retains her blue hair, and kneeling on the yellow earth, she joins in the evolutionary cycle in full awareness. Temperance pours her liquid from one pitcher to the other; the young woman of the Star puts it into circulation to nourish humanity. There is no longer any duality. The Star is united with the cosmos.

With the help of two red pitchers she pours the blue water of the invisible world into a lake, or even a river, the color of the sea and sky. Energy flows from the pitcher and spreads through the water, the mother of life, which diffuses knowledge and symbolizes psychism. Water has a purifying value; Hindus purify themselves in the water of the Ganges, and baptism in the waters of the Jordan cleanses all sin.

The Star is the first arcanum concerned with the sky and the cosmos. Up till now, the Magician was enclosed in his own universe, but with 17 he merges into the cosmic life and distributes the treasures gleaned along his hard but rewarding road. Now with the Star, man can no longer choose his path like the Lover; his destiny is marked out in the sky and the stars, which will lead him to Knowledge.

Kant said, "Two things fill me with admiration, the starry sky above me and the moral law within me." This card includes seven little stars that remind us of the Pleiades, and one large star, like the sun with sixteen rays of red and yellow. The Pleiades make the sign of their name in the constellation of Taurus.

Among the eight stars in arcanum 17, five have eight rays, the number of Justice. The two stars in the upper corner of the card have seven points, 7 being the addition of the square (4), solidly based in the manifest world, and the triangle (3), the essence and manifestation. These seven stars evoke the rainbow. The music of the spheres requires seven notes.

The large central star asks us to ally the active justice of its seven red rays with the contemplative justice of its seven yellow ones, in order to rise above dualism by the alchemical operation of the union of opposites, which creates the power of light. The Chaldeans considered the stars as gods. In their early writings, God was represented by the ideogram of an eight-pointed star, which later became the emblem of Ishtar, the divine but sensual warrior, dispenser of vital energy. It is this energy that the young women of the Star pours into the river, which will distribute its vital power around the world so that all the inhabitants may profit from it.

This star is also the double star of Venus, which lights up our nights by being the first to come out or the last to vanish after sunrise.

Placed after the most disturbing card of the Tarot, the Tower, the Star is one of the happiest cards, which leads to Hope, which might also be the name of this card. We cannot separate love from hope—the virtue that delivers us from evil, oppression, and injustice.

Perched upon a tree, which might be the Tree of the World, the Tree of Life, a black bird represents the celestial world in contrast to the snake, which represents the terrestrial world. In the Qur'an, the bird is the symbol of immortality of the soul. In the Upanishads, which express he essence of the Vedas, the origins of Hindu thought, two birds are perched on a similar tree. One is the soul, the other the Lord. They are the living symbols of divine thought and of the migration of the soul from body to body.

The Star is a return to the source. It is a card of good fortune, and it mitigates the effect of any ill-omened cards around it. At the worst, the Star may indicate a bad astrological period. It stands for harmony, hope, the end of an ordeal, a happy fate. Don't we say of someone fortunate that he was born under a lucky star? Astronomy is considered the mother of all the arts. The Star is the card of inspiration for artists, poets, musicians, astrologers. It is also the card of idealism, of happy nights, and of occult protection.

In the case of illness it brings hope of a cure and strength. It stands for a well-wisher and for first aid.

17, the number of the Star, is divisible only by 1 and itself. It therefore stands for isolation. Egyptian mythology puts the death of Osiris at the seventeenth day of the month of Athyr. In Islamic lore, there are seventeen *rak'a*—liturgical gestures—in the five daily prayers and seventeen words in the call to prayer.

When we look at the Star we think first of luck—of a very protective kind—and of hope and beauty, which are the salt of life.

The Moon

Positioned numerologically after the Star, this card continues the series of cosmic cards begun by 16, the Tower, which represents a link between heaven and earth. With card 18 we are in the cosmos.

The Moon, full and round, contains a crescent in the center of which can be seen a human face. Its rays light up the earth with their wan light. The upper portion represents the psychic side of the card, the moon of the mind. The planet is blue, the traditional color of spirituality, but also of immobility. Red, action, appears very little in this card. Blue is the color of heaven and of the sea; the glance loses itself in the infinity of blue, a cold, pure, unearthly color. Blue, like white, indicates a separation from earthly values, a closeness to God.

The middle of the card, which shows the material world, is yellow. Yellow, like gold, is the color of love. This yellow earth is dry, arid, encircled on each side by crenellated towers. These take us back to the Tower, struck by lightning.

In the depths of the lake, also blue, is a crayfish, emblem of the subterranean world, of man's examination of his conscience, which returns to its divine self. The crayfish recalls the sign of the Crab, which is the astrological dwelling-place of the moon. It possesses the same qualities and meanings. It devours everything that is corrupt and takes part in its regeneration. The crayfish periodically sheds it shell, like man, whose cells are renewed every seven years.

The dogs represent the Freudian libido, the psychic barrier. Traditionally they are the mediators between the physical and psychic worlds. The dog is linked to the vegetative and sexual life. It is a psycho-inflater, the bond between this world and the other, between the loving and the dead. The moon dogs are nourished by the energy that falls in droplets.

The Moon, the only card that does not contain any person, has nevertheless abundant symbolism. Its only light is the reflection of the sun, and as such is diffuse and wan. It is the perfect representation of the feminine principle and what flows from it. It is periodic cycles and continual renewal. It also stands for the impalpable part of a person, the secret garden, the unconscious and its association with night and dreams.

After the Star of the future, we see a return to the past, to the origins of life and our beginnings.

The Greeks called the moon Selene and considered it as the most important divinity after the sun. It was then put under the governance of Diana or Artemis, the twin of Apollo, the sun, with whom the world was alternately illuminated. She is also Hecate, the lunar goddess, linked to the cult of fertility, who presides over birth and germination but who also has a magical and witching aspect, the goddess of nocturnal apparitions, the hell of psychicism.

She is the eternal feminine, the divinity of woman. She is also Maya, or illusion. Maya, contrary to a popular misconception, does not signify that the world is an illusion. Rather the illusion comes only from our way of looking at things.

The lunar zone of a person is that of instinctive and often hidden impulses, of feelings. It leads the memory of night to the gleam of day and knowledge. It is nostalgia for the past. The Moon is the card of the visionary, of the artist, of poets and writers. It often foretells gestation or pregnancy. It also foretells, in association with other cards, errors of judgment, fraud, lies, a flight from truth, sometimes theft, illusion, doubt, and all bad influences.

Sometimes it indicates a tendency to obesity, ovarian or digestive problems, or lymphatic or psychic troubles.

We should never forget, with the moon, that water is a maternal element, symbol of birth, fertility, and creation. It is the most feminine of all signs. The man of the sign of Cancer, however virile he be, always seeks his mother in the women he loves. The Moon reminds us that the future flows from the past, that both are indissolubly tied together. We must overcome the past in order not to commit the same mistakes again.

The number 18 is made up of 1, the divine number, and 8, which represents the fall of the spiritual into matter. This matter afterward returns to the spiritual. Buddha meditated 4×7 days, or 28, the time of the lunar period, beneath the bodhi, the tree of knowledge, before he attained nirvana.

The Moon, like 18, is therefore the perfect representation of creation. She is passive, receptive, fertile, and she symbolizes night, dampness, the unconscious, the visionary. She is the door to heaven and to hell. She is the multitude, inspiration, intuition, prophecy, but also navigation.

As the moon reflects the sun's light, human intelligence reflects the creative light of knowledge.

The Sun

After the pallid light of the Moon, we are dazzled by the bright light of the Sun, a sun with a human face. It sparkles with sixteen rays, and we are thus reminded of the Tower, whose successor it is, proving that it was not so very formidable. The colors of its rays indicate that they operate in all realms. The Sun is at once the source of light and power and manna from heaven. This latter is symbolized by the drops that resemble golden rain, like that into which Jupiter was metamorphosed for the seduction of Danae and the fathering of Perseus.

The Sun is the emblem of Christ, of Buddha, of Vishnu, and of Apollo, the sun god. It is direct illumination, atman, the universal spirit. On one of the murals of the temple of Philae in Egypt, as on the door of the temple of Medina-Abu, can be read: "It is he, the sun, who has made all that there is and nothing has ever been made without him." The sun is the source of heat, of life; it symbolizes resurrection and immortality.

The two imps of arcanum 15 (the Devil), thrown to earth from the Tower, have learned their lesson well from their ordeals. They have become the twins onto whom the splashes of light fall. With bare torsos, dressed only in blue loin-cloths, they trap with their bare feet the yellow energy that rises from the earth. They have controlled their instincts and passions. They are at the same time Purusha and Prakriti, the brothers of Hindu mythology, and Castor and Pollux, the sons of Jupiter, hatched from the eggs of Leda, their mother.

The twins are also the persons in the egg of the Great Work, described in the *Mutus Liber*, the bible of the alchemists. These twins represent the essential duality always found in alchemy. The egg must undergo a multitude of processes so that the fixed matter it contains can become volatile. This volatility can in its turn become fixed, in order to attain the ultimate transformation.

We also find the concept of the primordial egg in the Vedas of India and in Eastern theogonies: The egg that floats on the water breaks its shell before multiplying and creating heaven and earth. We find this concept also in Orphism.

The yellow wall behind the twins encloses their universe by separating them from darkness, but it limits their activity. This red-bordered wall stops halfway up the twins' height in order to give them their own exact measure. The red stones of action are joined to those of the golden color of the sun. These stones, which already form a wall, will later serve for the erection of a new tower, a new temple, a new Jerusalem.

In alchemy, the sun is the beginning of the Red Work, Rubeo, the third part of the great philosophical work that produces the "powder of sympathy."

The sun symbolizes cosmic intelligence. Heliopolis, the city of the sun, played an important part in the religious history of Egypt. There Ra was worshiped, the rising, visible sun, later assimilated with Atum, the setting sun from whom Ra was born. Atum, god creator, was himself created before begetting Shu and Tefnut, with whom he formed a triad.

The cult of the sun, also called Helios, spread throughout the ancient world. The Greeks worshiped him and dedicated many altars to him.

The sun is the yang principle, masculine and active, in comparison to the moon, yin, feminine and passive. The moon disperses energy; the sun concentrates it. The moon favors inspiration; the Sun gives it being. The moon is the soul; the Sun is the spirit, the chief masculine generator, the husband, the father, the guide, the authority, the chief, the king, the emperor, the hero.

The Upanishads teach that the sun begets and devours its children. It is eternal creation. It is the triumph of matter, success, the joy of living, riches, friendship, a prestigious circle, conjugal harmony, knowledge, savoir faire.

The *Emerald Tablet* says, in speaking of the Superior Being, that "his father is the sun, his mother is the moon." This sun-moon duality is that of Vishnu and Shiva. We find it also in the trigrams Li and K'an, corresponding to the sun and the moon, in the I Ching, the book of Changes, whose origins go back to antiquity.

In astrology the sun symbolizes life, warmth, day, light, authority, everything that shines. It is the masculine generative principle, the father. It is also social constraint, the law, but most of all, it alone determines our astrological sign by its position at the moment of our birth. It is, then, above all the Self, the heart, vitality.

This card is always positive. In certain cases, it can indicate vanity, or showing off, the brilliance that blinds, but it is never a bad card, properly speaking. It leads to earthly happiness, happy love, harmony.

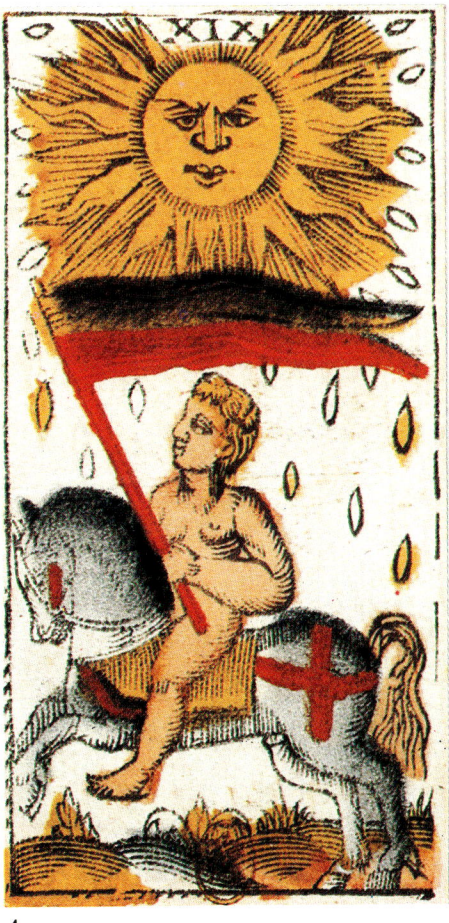

The Sun of the tarot deck has a human face. Here are examples from the Paris tarot (1), the Besançon tarot (2), the Rider-Waite deck (3), and the Vieville tarot (4). In the last we can discern influences from the tarot decks of Milan and Bologna. Source of heat and light, the Sun is a symbol of rebirth, immortality and cosmic intelligence. The Cult of the Sun was widespread in the ancient world. It determines our astrological sign. The Sun above all stands for the self, vitality and the masculine generative principle.

Judgment

Judgment is announced by an angel with a white halo, whose flesh-colored wings remind us of those of Temperance; like hers, they intervene in the material world because they are the color of matter. In some decks this card is called the Angel or the Trumpet. The Angel, made of the same material as man, shows that all can acquire the wings of spirituality if they know how to retain their balance while ascending.

The yellow hair reflects a sun symbol, but the blue cloud surrounding the angel is the moon's color. It is therefore associated with the spiritual world by blue, the color of the deepest truths of the soul. The spirals of the same color, which protect the angel by forming a circle difficult to penetrate, let through the yellow and red rays, for activity and intelligence. The left hand holds a white flag of purity with a yellow cross, a sign of unavoidable sacrifice. The sleeves are red, and therefore active; in the right hand is a trumpet directed toward the earth, perhaps meaning the Last Judgment.

The trumpet has always been an essential part of religious and public ceremonies. It joins heaven and earth in a common celebration and sends out the magic concentration of mystical contents.

An elderly man and a women are kneeling before what may be a tomb and looking intently at the spiritual and physical transmutation of a third person emerging from the tomb and standing naked before them. We see only the third person's back, so for us it is an androgynous figure in its duality. It is the Magician, the Lover, the Hanged Man, brought back from the dead like Lazarus or Christ. It is the resurrection of the flesh, but it is also a spiritual rebirth.

The neophyte undergoes many initiatory tests. Having passed through the last one successfully, he is welcomed by his teachers as their equal and reborn at last in the green sepulcher, a symbol of vitality and the color of the earthly paradise. Some initiations include a stay in a tomb as the final test.

The mystery religions—notably those of Eleusis—show man's hope for resurrection. The funeral ceremonies of ancient Egypt are based entirely on the idea of resurrection, an absolute sign of divine manifestation.

This arcanum ought to be called the Resurrection. However, it is called the Judgment because, according to tradition, the Last Judgment is not only a part of the resurrection, but is identified with it. It is not God who will judge men, but they themselves, for according to Saint John the Apostle, Jesus said, "Let him who is without sin among you cast the first stone." God does not wish to play the role of accuser. Each man will arrange his own trial and be his own judge. The reign of the spirit will be realized when humanity dwells in harmonious unity, with all cults and dogmas abandoned, thanks to universal love.

In this card, the angel is not a judge, but merely the herald who proclaims to man that it is time to survey his life and benefit from it. After his initiation through the arcana of the tarot, the Magician can see objectively, as in a mirror, what he has become. In truth, during the whole course of his existence, evolutionary man has never ceased judging himself; he constantly seeks justification for his deeds and his conduct.

We also find the ideal of man judging himself in the religious writings of the Egypt of the pharaohs and in *The Book of the Dead*. On the threshold of Amenti, where the tribunal of Osiris sits, the heart of the deceased is placed on the scale of Justice, to be weighed against Truth. The confession of the dead person would then decide whether his soul would enter paradise.

The Judgment is therefore the definitive victory over Maya (illusion). It is the final fulfillment of true knowledge, Gnosis. Man has torn away all the veils that shrouded his consciousness, and he knows himself at last, self-knowledge being the supreme end of ancient wisdom. He is in perfect communion with the Divine.

Judgment is the last ordeal; it is rebirth, brotherhood, reward, fame. It is a card of renewal, indicating the end of an illness, of a lawsuit, of a bad period. It means rehabilitation. It stands for beneficial words, divination, propaganda, the judgment of one's peers, triumph over an ordeal, yearly or cyclical rebirth, that is, springtime, Nature's awakening.

Badly placed, it may emphasize prattling nonsense, blunders that could have been avoided, noise, a deafening uproar, overexcitement, drunkenness, a lack of poise, a punishment.

It always proclaims a return to health.

Its number is 20, being the 2 of duality plus the 0 of infinity. The neophyte in the Judgment has found the two worlds he was seeking but could not attain; he has understood what the High Priestess was concealing, and lifting the veil at last he has found Knowledge.

The World

In contrast to the preceding cards, the World represents neither a scene nor a specific person, but diverse elements loosely connected.

In the center of a wreath of blue, red, and yellow flowers, a naked woman—or perhaps a hermaphrodite—dances on a yellow cloud. This wreath is shaped like a *mandorla*, an almond-shaped figure that usually contains representations of some holy figures such as Christ, the Virgin Mary, saints, or Hindu divinities in traditional iconography. The *mandorla* stands for the union of heaven and earth, the overlapping of dualities such as spirit-matter, or soul-body. It is paradise rediscovered, or nirvana, the perfect return to the infinite.

This garland is also the egg in which Brahma was born, the forebear of humanity according to the *Rig Veda*. The cosmic egg is a universal symbol of the world and its creation. We find the alchemical egg in the card of the Sun, at the same time the seat and the subject of transmutation. The first plate of the *Mutus Liber*, or *Secret Book* of alchemy, published in 1677, is illustrated with a wreath very like that in the World.

Two wands, like those of the Magician, represent opposing forces—positive and negative, yang and yin, masculine and feminine, united in the central figure who holds one in each hand.

This woman or hermaphrodite has only one leg touching the earth, the other being bent behind at a right angle in order to concentrate her powers as the Emperor and the Hanged Man have done. The figure dances rhythmically. The cosmic and religious dance is a rite of identification with the Creator and with creation, symbolic of God's action. Whirling dervishes achieve unity through their dancing, which enables them to rise toward God. To the Greeks and the Egyptians, rhythmic dancing celebrated legendary events and ritual feasts. The dance of the mythical gods brought them close to the creation and the cyclical destruction of the world.

The dance movement reminds us of the cosmic dance of Shiva, personification of a dynamic universe engaged in infinite motion: the dance of energy. Shiva's dance is the dance of subatomic matter, the dance of particles. Modern physics has shown us that motion is the essential property of matter. The *Bhagavad Gita* has Krishna say, "If I do not act, the worlds will perish."

At the four corners of this arcanum we can see the four evangelists hidden under their respective symbols. At the lower left, a horse or a bull represents the earth, the flesh. That is Saint Luke. The horse corresponds to the unconscious, the bull to creative power, to springtime; in the form of a calf it stands for sacrifice. On the lower right, matter evolves and becomes a lion, which means summer, fire, gold, intelligence, power. That is Saint Mark. He has a halo of flesh, and he is therefore in the world of matter but already on the spiritual path. On the upper right we find a yellow eagle, the color of the sun, with blue wings like those of Cupid, the Lover, and the Devil. The red halo stands for the spirit ruling instinct; it is air, rising upward, autumn. That is Saint John. Beside him to the left an angel with red wings, meaning the spirit in evolution. It is water, the scorpion, winter. It is Saint Matthew.

This card leads us to the Apocalypse of Saint John, in which he saw: "In the midst of the throne, and round about the throne were four beasts full of eyes before and behind. And the first beast was like a lion, and the second like a calf, and the third had a face as a man, and the fourth was like a flying eagle."

The realization attained in the Judgment finds its synthesis in the World, arriving at a supreme unity. The Magician comes to the end of his road of initiation. He has reached a balance of inner forces by taking the royal road, that of the tarot.

The World is the most prestigious arcanum; it is both its summary and its end. Nostradamus had drawn this card on the wall of his room, and from it derived divinatory knowledge.

The World is seldom a bad omen; even when badly placed it encourages us not to lose hope, but to keep faith in eternal regeneration.

Its number is 21, or 3 x 7, the number of perfection in the Bible. Wisdom has twenty-one attributes. 21 symbolizes divine wisdom, the mirror of eternal light. It stands for the dynamic effort to the new man who slowly works free from the struggle of opposites that torment him.

The World is therefore achievement, perfect knowledge, utter peace, the cosmos, supreme elevation. On the material plane it indicates success, the consummation of a work, an aerial voyage, a stranger. It corresponds to the Greater Fortune of the geomancers, in comparison to the Lesser Fortune of the Wheel of Fortune. It is apotheosis.

The Fool

It would have been quite normal if our journey through the tarot had ended with the World, the arcanum of perfection confirmed by the number 21, the number that has in itself the value of achievement. But there is another arcanum, and it is remarkable for being the only one that does not have a number.

This card is called the Fool and sometimes the Madman and sometimes, but rarely, the Vagabond, merely to confuse us. The person represented walks, like Death, toward the right, a sign of creative action, confirmed by his clothing, in which the blue of spirituality and the yellow of intelligence are mingled. His little blue cape has fool's bells, five of them, the number of man. He leans on a staff, as the Hermit does, but in a different sense. The Fool turns his back on the world in order to follow his personal path, because he knows the secrets of life, but he feels the need to synthesize them, and that is why he goes alone, like Moses to Mount Horeb.

His beggar's wallet, the color of flesh, is his last earthly possession, containing a slender crop of feelings, thoughts, and remembrances. The quantity is small because the Fool has found little in this world, and truth, like happiness, lies in simple values and few encumbrances.

A flesh-colored cat, reflecting the aggressiveness of certain animals, claws at the Fool's breeches, but he pays no attention. He reminds us of the Arabian proverb: "The dogs bark; the caravan passes." The Fool already has his eyes fixed on another world, and the indignities of this one do not bother him.

The tufts of grass scattered on the ground, the color of light and intelligence, are five in number—always the number of man—but the white tufts dominate; the Fool's aspirations therefore are more spiritual than material.

In French, this card is called Le Mat. We really do not know the origin of the name of this person who, in the game of chess, checkmates the King. Does he come from the Arabic word signifying death, or from *matto*, meaning mad in Italian? Both are plausible and in harmony with the meaning of this arcanum, in which the personage may be dead to this world; he therefore has the value of 0, which is the one usually given to him. However, he is made in the same way as was Don Quixote, that generous and nobly foolish knight. He is also the king's jester dressed in the buffoon's costume. Because he was outside the rules, that fool could speak with impunity of truths that were not always wise to speak. "To appear mad is the secret of wise men," said Aeschylus. Mercury, an indispensable element of alchemy, is called the fool of the Great Work because of its inconsistency and solubility.

The Fool is man who has passed through all the stages of evolution and who has arrived at a higher level. He is therefore as far removed from the

---

With the Magician—Original inspiration

With the High Priestess—A secret revealed

With the Empress—A scientific discovery

With the Emperor—Power in incompetent hands

With the Hierophant—A false prophet, an uncontrolled mystical impulse

With the Lovers—A bad choice

With the Chariot—A lack of realism in plans and ambitions

With Justice—Danger in legal matters

With the Hermit—Ideas and research should seek a new direction

With the Wheel of Fortune—Big changes in the offing

With Strength—Beware of a foolish act

With the Hanged Man—Freedom is threatened; prison is possible

With Death—The threat of ruin

With Temperance—Talent and sometimes even genius

With the Devil—Perhaps megalomania but always tyranny

With the Tower—Beware of lack of balance, psychic as well as physical

With the Star—Inspiration but spiced with risk

With the Moon—Deranged imagination: perhaps mythomania or other mental illness

With the Sun—Risk of a dangerous calamity

With Judgment—Scorn for public opinion

With the World—Overweening ambition or possibly a sudden impulsive departure reasoning of other humans as those who do not understand him. Since the Fool has crossed the threshold between the two worlds, he no longer sees the earthly life from the same point of view. Like Lao-tzu, he thinks that "the further one goes, the less one knows." In the first Epistle to the Corinthians, Saint Paul says, "Let no man deceive himself. If any man among you seemeth to be wise in this world, let him become a fool, that he may be wise. For the wisdom of this world is foolishness with God." Human reasoning in effect leads to a philosophical impasse, because it cannot imagine a God who is not like itself.

En Soph, the primordial point, infinity, the Creator in *Zohar*, cannot be named or imagined. When man considers the gulf between himself and God he is overcome. "What is man in infinity?" the Fool asks himself, a forerunner of Blaise Pascal, unable to "know with certainty, or to be totally unaware."

The Fool is the initiate who has passed the test of complete humility because he does not delude himself about the relative state of his knowledge, and his reason does not give him any certainty. He thought to find and to understand, but he knows now that he must seek further. Life slumbers in the mineral world, awakens in the vegetable, becomes organized in the animal, and analyzes itself in the human, and then, suddenly, beyond the human, it finds the Great Unknown. Man must wander in the night hoping that his evolution will allow him to attain the supreme Wisdom. Montesquieu wrote that "as there are many wise things that have led to great foolishness, so there are also many foolish ones that have led to great wisdom."

It is the Fool's freedom that allows him to go forward. This card is the one of irrationality, irrationality before birth and after death. It is also the card of Wisdom. This Fool warns us against the wandering of the spirit and advises us not to stray outside our limitations. It indicates indifference, freedom, chance, but also unreasonable impulses, unexpected disturbances, the unreasonable, estrangement, the lack of practical sense, vagrancy, and disillusion.

Although it represents the twenty-second card of the tarot, the Fool has 0 value because it does not count by itself. However, since 0 is nothing by itself but reinforces another number placed before it, it affects other cards; it changes the meaning of each card as soon as it is added to it (see the table).

This irrational Fool comes after each card whose end it is. It can be everywhere and nowhere, it has no set place in the order of the Arcana; it is always unpredictable and unexpected.

The Fool goes beyond the rational to go beyond itself, so that eventually it may meet the Absolute. It renounces human wisdom after having submitted to it during its initiation. It must now renounce what it has acquired and transcend its knowledge in total freedom.

Thus, the Fool concludes the tarot, returning endlessly in an infinite round, the round of life.

Beauty of design and harmonious coloring are also to be found on the backs of the tarot cards. Here, the reverse of the famous pack of Mademoiselle Lenormand.

The Major Arcana Speak to Us

The most beautiful experience we can have is that of mystery.
—Albert Einstein

It is clear that meaning of a particular card is altered by its neighbors. Several volumes would not suffice to list all the possible combinations; however, when one has taken the time to study a particular card, the signification that it takes on in relationship to its neighbors begins to reveal itself.

Relationships Between Cards in the Major Arcana

First one must study a card, its figures, its colors, its number, and then compare it to the cards that accompany or surround it. One will discover identical details and colors, a symbolism that indicates very clearly whether cards complement or oppose each other.

The ramifications of these juxtapositions can seem rather complex at first, but as we familiarize ourselves with the symbolism of each card their various relations will begin to unfold. As we advance in our study of the tarot, our responsiveness to them deepens. The cards become ever more suggestive.

Nostradamus said, "The gift of prophecy is a dynamic and powerful virtue that manifests itself as a beam of sunlight, which is showered on simple and complex beings." We must open ourselves to this sunlight that is the understanding of the tarot. The study and contemplation of each of the major arcana educates our imagination and enables us to receive this revelation that comes from beyond ourselves. This beyond exists neither in time nor in space but rather in that Absolute of which Swami Vivekananda speaks in his *Jnana Yoga*. This Absolute, unconditioned by time, space, or causality, can be seen as through a glass.

Let us try to think of the symbolism of the tarot in this way, as portents from beyond the realm of our senses: Matthew, Isaiah, and Ezekiel all insisted: "They have eyes, but they see not." We must open our eyes to discern our destiny—or that of others, which is considerably easier—inscribed in the space-time continuum. We must allow the awareness that goes beyond ordinary reality to cross the threshold of our consciousness.

First we must distinguish between the cards in the major arcana. There are the cards that have a determining and creative value: the Hierophant, Justice, the Hermit, Strength, Death, the Devil, the Tower. Then there are cards that bring about changes in that which already exists: the Lovers, the Chariot, the Wheel of Fortune, the Star, Judgment, the World, and the Fool. Finally there are cards that are essentially dependent on others: the Magician, the High Priestess, the Empress (representing the female consultant), the Emperor (the male consultant), the Hanged Man, Temperance, and the Moon.

On the following page there appears a list of the meanings of several cards in combination. But one must always view these within the total context of the reading.

This list simply gives us an indication of the semantic richness that resides in the arcana. It is meant only to suggest the multiplicity of possibilities that are born out of the relationship of one card with another. Of course, we must bear in mind that the relationship is modified when a third card is added. And it goes without saying that the possible resonances and interconnections brought about by adding a fourth card lead to almost infinite possibilities of interpretation.

In any event, one must not seize upon a rigid or predetermined sense of each of the arcana. The symbolism of each card can have many different applications, depending upon the situation under consideration. This exercise will turn out to be quite easy if the reader is

Judgment from the tarot of Charles VI. At the sound of the trumpets of the Last Judgment, the dead rise from their graves. The body is transformed into spirit in preparation for rebirth. For alchemy, the last stage that reunites body, mind, and spirit.

possessed of some psychic gifts, which is true more often than one might think. In effect we all have a degree of prescience, which we have buried in our consciousness. It need only be made manifest.

One often meets people who confess, after an event that had a powerful impact on their lives, that they had a presentiment that they were reluctant to admit. They were practically sure of what was to come but brushed this awareness aside for any one of a dozen reasons.

The practice of reading the tarot, connected as it is to meditation, permits the development of that intuition that, all unknown to us, sleeps in our unconscious, only to appear from time in a fashion that is unexpected and uncontrolled but leaves a mark difficult to erase.

THE MAGICIAN with THE HIGH PRIESTESS . . . Pregnancy

THE MAGICIAN with THE CHARIOT . . . Progress

THE MAGICIAN with THE HANGED MAN, DEATH, or THE TOWER . . . Resumption of activity after a check

THE MAGICIAN with THE STAR . . . A favorable period. Do not lose any time.

THE HIGH PRIESTESS with THE HIEROPHANT or THE LOVERS . . . Pregnancy or a meeting concerning some secret affair

THE HIGH PRIESTESS with JUSTICE . . . An equitable resolution to a difficult matter or a hidden element in a lawsuit

THE HIGH PRIESTESS with THE HANGED MAN . . . Halt in activity due to pregnancy

THE HIGH PRIESTESS with DEATH or THE TOWER . . . Risk of miscarriage

THE HIGH PRIESTESS with THE DEVIL . . . Sexual problems for a woman or something hidden concerning money or power

THE HIGH PRIESTESS with THE MOON . . . Pregnancy or a train of troubling events

THE HIGH PRIESTESS with THE WORLD . . . A birth or the publication of a book

THE HIEROPHANT with JUSTICE . . . A judge or counselor in a legal matter

THE LOVERS with THE HIEROPHANT . . . A meeting that leads to marriage

THE LOVERS with JUSTICE . . . Hesitation in a legal matter

THE LOVERS with THE DEVIL . . . A romantic encounter with strong physical attraction

THE CHARIOT with THE LOVERS . . . A journey for the purpose of lovemaking

THE CHARIOT with THE HANGED MAN, DEATH, or THE TOWER . . . Need for great caution when traveling by car

THE CHARIOT with JUDGMENT or THE WORLD . . . Victory achieved

JUSTICE with THE HIEROPHANT . . . A legal agreement

JUSTICE with THE DEVIL . . . A lawsuit concerning money

JUSTICE with THE STAR, THE SUN, or JUDGMENT . . . Victory in a legal matter

JUSTICE with THE WORLD . . . Contract with a foreigner

THE HERMIT with THE HANGED MAN . . . Enforced solitude, obstacles

THE HERMIT with THE TOWER . . . Danger of an operation or accident

THE HERMIT with THE MOON . . . Pay attention to a hidden ailment

THE HANGED MAN with THE TOWER . . . Possible paralysis due to an accident

THE DEVIL with THE TOWER . . . Loss of Money

THE DEVIL with THE MOON . . . Beware of swindlers and thieves

THE MOON with THE HANGED MAN . . . Forced immobilization due to pregnancy or a hidden ailment

THE SUN with THE LOVERS . . . A great love

THE SUN with THE WORLD . . . A wonderful journey

Methods of Reading

There exist numerous ways to read the tarot. In fact anyone can invent his own; the light that the reading sheds on the situation under consideration will be the same.

Arrangement in the form of a cross

The simplest arrangement, especially when it is a question of a specific inquiry, is that of a cross constructed of five cards. First one should choose a card to represent the situation to be elucidated. The list below indicates the general situations to which each of twenty-one major arcana corresponds. (The Fool is not used for this purpose.)

One next places the card that has been chosen to represent the situation in the center of the cross. The card above will comment generally on the situation; the card below will be its meaning. At the left is what is in favor of a successful resolution; to the right, what opposes it. One may then add a final card above to the right, to foretell the result (see arrangement below). In this reading one must not overlook the cards that are "for" and "against." If there is a doubt about the meaning of a card one may place another on top of it for clarification. At the outset, however, one ought to avoid using too many cards as there is a danger that rather than helping one better understand this can muddy the waters.

In arranging the cards one can either lay them all face

THE MAGICIAN . . . A birth or new departure

THE HIGH PRIESTESS . . . A pregnancy or literary creation

THE EMPRESS . . . Concerning a woman

THE EMPEROR . . . Concerning a man

THE HIEROPHANT . . . Education

THE LOVERS . . . Romance

THE CHARIOT . . . A voyage on land

JUSTICE . . . A legal process

THE HERMIT . . . A radical change or an osteopathic condition

THE WHEEL OF FORTUNE . . . Chance

STRENGTH . . . Courage or physical resistance

THE HANGED MAN . . . An obstacle or the circulatory system

DEATH . . . A doctor or lawyer

TEMPERANCE . . . Communication, a telephone call

THE DEVIL . . . Money, sex, power

THE TOWER . . . Change of residence or an operation

THE STAR . . . Arts, music, a happy period

THE MOON . . . The home or a fraud

THE SUN . . . Love, success

JUDGMENT . . . Conferences or all that concerns language

THE WORLD . . . A voyage by air

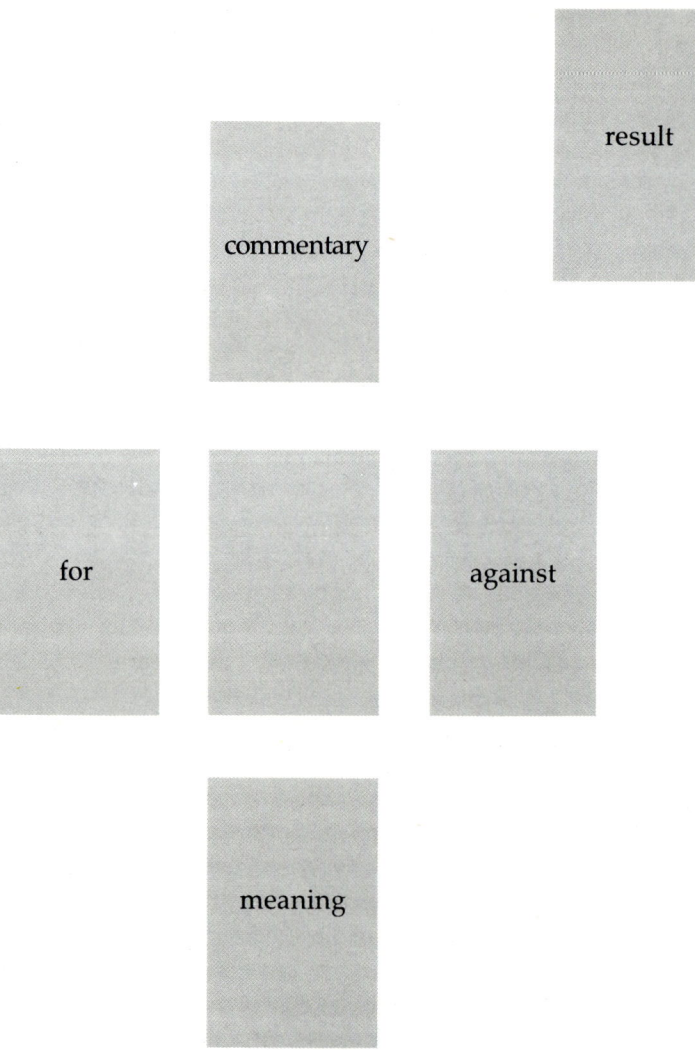

(*Preceding page*) Predicting the future with cards in the second empire (*La Cartomancienne*, Musée Carnavalet). (*Opposite*) Cover of a popular book. Chiromancy has existed since the dawn of time, whereas cartomancy has imposed itself, as a support for clairvoyance, since the eighteenth century. The word *support* indicates that the playing cards are simply instruments that enable the exercise of psychic gifts.

down and choose them at random or cut the cards, shuffle them well, and deal them off the top of the pack. Either way will yield successful results.

One can further refine the response by placing on top of the cards from major arcana, the minor arcana selected in the same fashion. But one can obtain extremely subtle and insightful readings using the major arcana exclusively.

Arrangement in a row of seven

Another way of reading that yields extremely interesting results is an arrangement with seven cards. It can be used as effectively to answer a particular question as to provide a general overview of the near future.

One first takes a card that pertains to the situation (as in the preceding reading in the form of the cross) or the

Emperor, if the consultant is male, or the Empress, if female. One then lays down six cards in row, face down. One turns over the cards one after another counting five from the first card (which one must always count). In this fashion one determines the progression of the situation. The last card (the seventh) turned over will be the card in the middle. (See the sample row of seven cards on page 62.)

Arrangement in three rows of three

This reading will help us foresee what the next three months will bring.

One lays down nine cards in three rows of three. The first row represents the first month; the second, the second month; the third, the third month.

Arrangement by astrological houses

This reading corresponds to the twelve astrological houses. It is arranged in the shape of a star with twelve points.

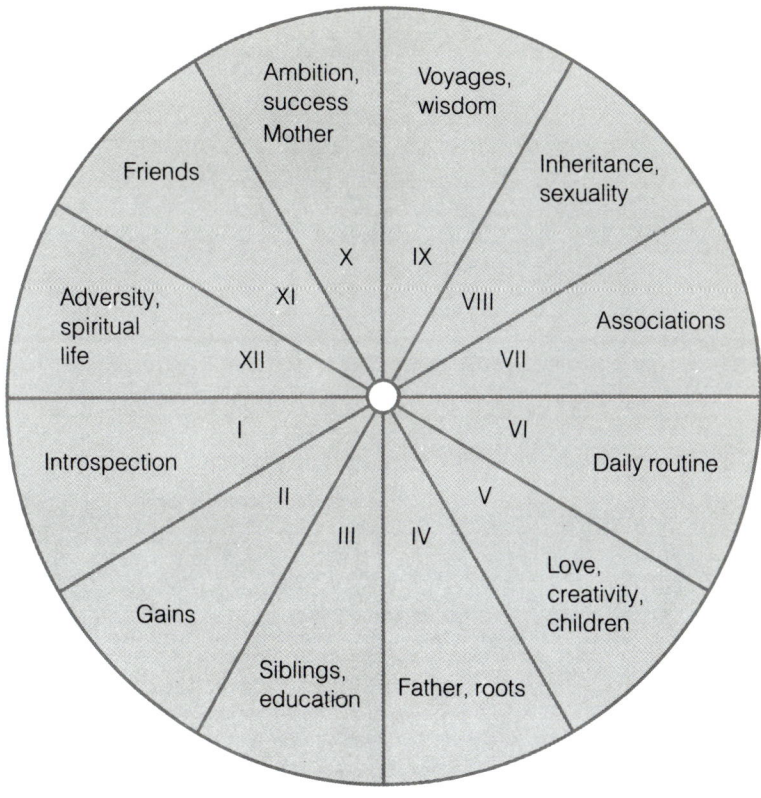

HOUSES	ATTRIBUTES
FIRST HOUSE...	Self, personality, introspection
SECOND HOUSE...	Profits, acquisitions, possessions
THIRD HOUSE...	Education, writing, brothers and sisters
FOURTH HOUSE...	Roots, childhood, family hearth, the father
FIFTH HOUSE...	Creativity in work or love, or children
SIXTH HOUSE...	Daily routine, minor illnesses and cares
SEVENTH HOUSE...	Others, associations, contracts, marriage
EIGHTH HOUSE...	Death, inheritance, sexuality
NINTH HOUSE...	Travel, foreigners, wisdom, philosophy
TENTH HOUSE...	Ambition, success, the mother
ELEVENTH HOUSE...	Friends, partnerships
TWELFTH HOUSE...	Isolation, retreat, imprisonment or hospitalization, adversity, but also the hidden life of hermits and mystics

One begins by laying down the cards, starting from the 9-o'clock position, counterclockwise, forming an astrological wheel.

The cards thus arranged will give us a picture of what we can expect in the various aspects represented by the astrological houses. It is possible to obtain further elucidation of a particular house by also laying down two or three cards from the minor arcana. This will clarify obscure significations.

In practicing any one of these methods, the student will soon find that it is possible to make his own modifications to these forms to address certain questions or reflect personal sensitivities.

The possibility of invention is limitless. Simply remove the constraints from the imagination, do not seek to impede its wandering and be willing to seize any new idea that arises.

(*Opposite*) The backs of tarot cards are often as striking as the faces. The four examples shown here demonstrate their diversity. From left to right: Deck of Jaro (André-Voisin), of Mademoiselle Lenormand, the Epinal tarot, and the Great Deck of Bellini.

The Minor Arcana

Hundreds of people can talk for one who can think, but thousands can think for one who can see.

—John Ruskin

The minor arcana consist of fifty-six cards divided into four suits. There is no evidence to suppose that the twenty-two major and fifty-six minor arcana derive complete from one original deck of seventy-eight cards. On the contrary, it is assumed that the figured and numbered cards of the minor arcana were developed independent of and at a later stage than the major arcana.

The Suits

There are four suits: swords, which correspond to spades; staves, or clubs; cups, or hearts; coins, or diamonds. There are many theories about their meaning. Several authors suggest that they represent the four seasons or the four elements, earth, water, fire, and air. Swords correspond to air, staves to fire, cups to water, and coins to earth. It is also possible that the suits correspond to the four divisions of medieval society, which existed at their conception. According to this schema swords would represent the knights and the nobility; staves, the peasant class; cups, the clergy; and coins, the emerging bourgeoisie. Certain other authors couple swords with justice, staves with power, cups with faith, and coins with charity.

Swords

Swords symbolize energy, bravery, and victory but also war and conflict. The sword has a double function: It stands for justice but also for destruction. In the Hindu tradition Vishnu carries a flaming sword with which he combats ignorance. The angels that drove Adam and Eve from paradise carried swords of fire. In the I Ching, the classic oracle of China, the trigram li corresponds to both the sun and the sword. The knights and heroes of the *Chansons de geste* all bore noble swords, which they named and which they used to vanquish evil and establish the order of chivalry. However, the sword is also an instrument of death. In the Bible Jeremiah cites it as one of the three scourges: hunger, pestilence, and the sword. In the major arcana justice wears a sword. In general swords announce conflict, obstacles, and difficulty.

Staves

Staves have a creative and ruling function. The stave is a weapon, as in Hindu iconography, where one finds it in the hands of many puissant divinities, and also a symbol of authority and sovereignty. It represents legitimacy and sometimes can be regarded as a scepter. It can also represent the teacher that guides us or the foundation upon which we can rely. Finally it is the sign of the initiate, as in the staff of Aesclepius or of Moses or that of the Hermit in the major arcana. The stave pertains primarily to action, work, and intelligence.

Cups

Cups represent the passive and receptive principle. The immediate association with the cup is the Grail, the chalice in which Joseph of Arimathea collected the blood of Christ. The quest for the Holy Grail figures importantly in the corpus of medieval literature. This cup, which contains blood, the life principle, represents the heart. The Egyptian hieroglyph for the heart is a vase, and this fact is confirmed by the mystical literature of Islam, in which the heart is often referred to as a cup.

The cup is also the symbol of the cosmic egg divided into two parts. The cup, then, corresponds to the heart and to the emotions.

The Page of Coins (Visconti-Sforza deck) announces news given in confidence of new ideas; its meaning will vary depending on the influences surrounding it. This card points to reflection, meditation, and erudition but also to a lack of coherence in one's ideas.

The King of Coins (Epinal deck) is a man of means. Though possessed of a strong sense of family, he disdains sentimentality.

The King of Swords (Arista deck) is a forceful, dominating personality: Given his strength and determination, it is best to have him as a friend.

Coins

Coins suggest wheels, symbols of continual creation, of the cyclical renewal, but in the minor arcana they uniquely concern the material domain: They rule business, commerce, money, and all that flows from these—ambition, hard work, and the desire for dominance. The physical ramifications of the other three suits work themselves out in coins.

Face Cards of the Minor Arcana

The Kings

The king is the archetype of human success. He can be many things: sage, guide, hero, father, but also cruel tyrant. The primal function of the king is to dispense justice and ensure the peace of the realm.

The three kings who recognized in Jesus the messiah, king of the world, brought presents to do him honor. In Egypt the pharaoh was identified with the sun and with the divine. In Chinese the character for king, *wang*, is formed by three parallel lines joined by a vertical stroke, imaging the king as an earthly presence invested with a portion of divinity. In Java and Angkor the king was given the title *chakravati*, universal monarch, un-

---

THE MODERN DECK OF PLAYING CARDS

Our deck of cards is derived from the fifty-six cards of the minor arcana. The four suits have been retained, transformed into spades, clubs, hearts, and diamonds. The knights, however, have been eliminated, or rather combined with the pages. reducing the final count to fifty-two, the number of weeks in a year.

The playing deck we know has forty numbered cards and twelve face cards, which suggest the twelve signs of the zodiac and the twelve months of the year. Accompanying these are one or more jokers. The joker is clearly a descendant of the Fool of the major arcana.

The King of Cups (Besançon deck) represents a fair-skinned, cultivated gentleman with a strong artistic bent. He is a good friend and valuable adviser.

The King of Staves (Paris deck) is a person of influence, sometimes a foreigner, often dark-haired, who is accustomed to command.

moved mover, situated in the emptiness in the hub of the cosmic wheel. According to Taoism, it is this emptiness that permits the wheel to turn and, in so doing, ensures the perpetual renewal of life.

The king is the image of the ideal one hopes to realize, the mastery of self one needs to acquire, the conscience and consciousness one strives to develop.

The King of Swords is above all intellectual, deeply involved in day-to-day struggle, be it in business, law, medicine, or politics. He is active, intelligent, courageous, and skilled, but he can be aggressive. In his right hand he holds the sword of power in which resides his creative force, but in his left hand lies a dagger with which he can just as easily destroy the creations of others. He does not fear attack; he knows how to defend himself.

He shows us the power of the mind. Ideas burgeon forth. His word is decisive; he moves in socially influential spheres and makes his own law. But fortune does not always smile upon his efforts in society.

He is competent, experienced, authoritarian, demanding. He also has a sense of thrift. His lack of scruples gives him great freedom of movement and power to be reckoned with. It is difficult to detect in him any weakness, an Achilles' heel. His conscience is somewhat elastic, and he knows how to extricate himself from difficult situations. He is well protected in his armor. His analytical capacities are formidable. He can be a powerful friend but also pitiless and a terrible enemy.

His presence announces tempests and storms and all the powers of the air.

The King of Staves is a person of influence, sometimes from a foreign land, usually brown haired. He is honest and conscientious, energetic, endowed with the air of command. He can be over-conventional or paternalistic

68

Captions 1 to 4 belong to the Tzigone tarot created by Tcholai, a descendant of this very ancient people of Rajputna in the north of India. Each card has a double meaning: It is divinatory in one sense, but in another it recounts the history of the Gypsies. 1. The battle of Taraim recalls the combat of the Rom with the Muslim invaders of the twelfth century. 2. Crowned with the helmets of Rajput princes, the Koukhan represent members of the warrior caste, the Kshatriya. 3. The Wheel of Origination is the emblem of liberty; it recalls the earrings worn by Gypsy women. 4. The Brotherhood of the Rom depicts their four tribes. Ten minor arcana (Besançon deck) and their divinatory sense. 5. The Ace of Swords possesses overpowering energy; it commands and conquers. 6. The 2 of Swords indicates major conflicts; we may discover that we are our own adversary. 7. The 3 of Swords engenders a darkened atmosphere, danger to one's health, aborted projects. 8. The 4 of Swords signifies a period of repose to gather up our strength. 9. The 5 of Swords tells us to remain vigilant to secure the victory we seek. 10. The 6 of Swords rewards past efforts. 11. The 7 of Swords brings hope if we rely on ourselves and not on chance. 12. The 8 of Swords indicates sadness and discord. 13. The 9 of Swords expresses grief. It is the most ill-omened card of the minor arcana. 14. The 10 of Swords evokes that which flourishes in darkness.

1. The Queen of Swords (Visconti-Sforza deck) is a dark-haired woman, divorced or widowed, free and of independent means. She is a positive force unless surrounded by unfortunate cards.

2. The Queen of Cups (Vieville deck) is usually blonde. She dwells in the midst of a family she cherishes. Intuitive rather than intellectual, she has a passionate and loving nature.

3. The Queen of Coins (Besançon deck) is a very accomplished woman. She enjoys arranging parties and charity balls. Despite an apparent superficiality, she is in reality quite sensitive to others' problems.

on occasion. He is generous but proud. In most instances he signifies a married man well brought up, a man of strong principles. He inspires confidence by his skillfulness and ability to get things done. His maturity, wisdom, and accessibility can be of great aid to those under his protection or for those to whom he vouchsafes his friendship. His remarkable intelligence serves him well in a wide range of endeavors.

He foretells a period of uninterrupted activity, of important dealings, of unlooked-for events, and often of great assistance in all undertakings.

He is also the harbinger of all things to do with the element fire: electrical storms, conflagrations and explosions.

The King of Cups is above all things flexible, easygoing, and sensitive. Although in the prime of life, he often appears younger on account of his optimism and gaiety. Generally he has blond hair. A man of learning, he has a strong artistic bent. He is often quite religious and open to new and unconventional ideas. His indulgence of others is at times carried too far and becomes a kind of weakness. This weakness exists for him on the physical plane as well. He lacks fortitude; his organism sometimes lacks the strength to obey his will. Because of this physical vulnerability and lack of endurance he often seems passive, resigned to his fate. He is incapable of sustained action or the perseverance required to bring ideas and projects to fruition.

Despite all this, one can always rely upon his benevolence, good counsel, practical ideas, professional experience, and sense of good fellowship. He gets carried away now and then but soon regains his sense of proportion.

The King of Coins is a successful businessman or a rich property holder. Most of all he knows how to make and keep his money. He knows well how to amass a fortune, less well how to dispense it. He is an intelligent executive who is skillful at negotiations and investments. He owes his success only to himself and to his talents for producing and saving. He is often endowed with great mathematical abilities and can reach the summits of that discipline. He is patient, hardworking and willing to take risks, but interested only in material things. The arts hold no attraction for him; he scoffs at intuition and detests anything that smacks of the irrational.

He has, however, a great love of nature, the earth, and all its products. Gardener or farmer, he will tend the soil with patience and diligence. A faithful husband, he has a strong sense of responsibility to the family. However, his is not a passionate nature, and sentimentality is not his strong suit.

This card foretells earthquakes, landslides, and avalanches.

The Queens

The queen is the king's companion, his complement on the symbolic plane. She possesses all the plenitude of the feminine: sweetness, emotional depth, tenderness, sensitivity, and understanding. The queen is the pivotal piece in the game of chess. She has more charm than reason, but she represents the culmination of feminine expressiveness. The rose is queen of flowers, that is, the most beautiful. The queen bee alone has the power to procreate in the hive. The moon is queen of the night, because its incomparable light illuminates the darkness. Without Mary, queen of heaven, Christ could not have been incarnated. The primordial function of the queen is to assure the perpetuity of the crown by providing an heir to the throne, a function second only to the governance on which its power is founded. Thus, upon her fragile shoulders rests the burden of continuation of the reigning line.

The knights of the middle ages, champions of good in its struggle against evil, noble and generous defenders of the right, often carried their queen's colors in tournaments or into battle and were willing to die for them.

The queen is a resplendent and majestic figure but can also represent vanity and dangerous seductiveness.

The Queen of Swords is a solitary and independent woman. She can be widowed or divorced. She is usually brown haired. Her life alone does not trouble her; just the contrary, in fact. She loves to be alone, to live without constraint. She is secretive, aloof, mysterious. Her past is well concealed, as are her emotions. She can appear hard at first, but her reserved charm will captivate whoever has the good fortune to get to know her well.

She possesses firm ideas and will not easily be distracted from the realization of her goals. She is always alert. She is highly intelligent. In certain cases in proximity to cards of evil omen, she becomes dangerous or cruel or perhaps shrewish. In general she is of serious demeanor, powerfully perceptive. Her penetrating eye scrutinizes you, as if seeing right into your soul, and she will render a strict and clear judgment. She can perceive others' intentions and at the same time analyze them with remarkable acuity.

The Queen of Staves is the incarnation of feminine grace and subtle charm. She is an independent and able woman of the world, intelligent and sympathetic, who takes a real interest in the welfare of others and can

The Knight of Cups (Paris deck) is a seducer. He announces a voyage of romance or a romantic encounter.

render them great services. She is also a devoted and sincere friend whose advice, opinions, and general good sense ought not be ignored.

She displays great intelligence in her circle, possessed of both fierce energy and serene authority. She very rarely signifies bad tidings, except when she is surrounded by negative influences, and even then her power to harm is extremely limited. She is an excellent mother and enjoys all the domestic arts. She is virtuous, chaste, generous, honorable, at her worst perhaps a bit jealous or proud. Although impatient with obstacles, she knows well how to adapt herself to changing circumstances.

Endowed with a vibrant personality, she personifies sweetness and grace. She never stands still.

The Queen of Cups is a good friend, a good wife, and a good mother. She knows well how to bring up and educate children. She is most often blonde. She loves company and will go to great lengths to avoid being alone or abandoned. She is usually surrounded by friends who make much of her and to whom she is generous to a fault. She is loving and amiable, sociable, devoted to her friends, and very giving. She likes to stay indoors and is comfortable in social settings. She loves poetry as much as she loves dreaming. Passionate and romantic, she is in her element in all that concerns love and lovers.

Intuitive rather than intellectual, she can be very acute, always imaginative, sometimes even clairvoyant. At the same time she is practical and honest. This card depends much on its surroundings, which will determine whether her influence is positive or negative. On balance, though, her presence is auspicious.

She is not bound by the strictest codes of morality, but with her all proceeds from the emotion of love, which makes itself felt all around her.

The Queen of Coins is no intellectual—her intelligence is, in fact, unremarkable—but she has excellent taste and is the perfect hostess. Her strengths easily lead one to overlook her weaknesses. She is often found organizing parties, which for her is generally quite easy, since she is rich and generous and enjoys society. She has done well in marriage, and her substantial means allow her to thrive in the luxurious surroundings she likes so well. She is ambitious but lacking in foolish vanity.

She can appear frivolous but is for the most part sensible and does not put on great airs. Her emotional resources are immense, and she has a generous heart. She wants those around her to partake of good cheer and has perhaps a weakness for drink. She also runs the risk of abusing drugs.

Most often her sensual nature is held in check by her dignity and respectability. Her greatest gift is in raising children. Her practical and generous spirit assures the comfort and security of all those within her circle.

The Knights

The knight above all is a valorous and triumphant rider. He knows how to control his steed and, together with him, seeks to do battle with the powers of evil. At the break of day, off to pursue some wild quest, the horse gallops as if blind and is guided by his rider. In the depth of the night when the knight is injured or lost, his horse knows the way, in turn directing his master. If there is division and conflict between horse and rider, their way can lead to death, but if there is communion and a sense of joint purpose, theirs is a wonderful journey that will lead eventually to triumph. Thus, the fate of the horse is inseparable from that of man.

As archetype, the horse bears death but also life. He is the incarnation of speed and strength, passing like

The Knight of Coins (Rider-Waite deck) does not stir up events. He allows developments to take their own course and knows how to profit by them.

lightning. The knight, be he soldier or hero, represents perfected self-mastery. Mounted in full battle dress on his charger, Saint Michael, patron saint of the chivalric order, fells the demon, just as Saint George slays the dragon.

The four horsemen of the Apocalypse carry the four terrors, and ruin and despair follow in their wake. But Christ, riding a white horse, accompanied by the celestial armies, also mounted on white steeds, overcomes the four horsemen utterly. All the great messianic figures are pictured on horseback to signify their high estate.

The knight stands for a vigorous young man with all the vigor, impetuousness, and creative power of youth. He announces traveling and changes of residence.

The audacity of the Knight of Swords is seductive but often marred by excessive egotism. He is fearless and heeds neither obstacles nor enemies. Unhesitatingly he charges right at his opponent, then wheels for a second onslaught. He can cause a lot of damage, sometimes to innocent bystanders. He has a strong intelligence, and his projects are original and worth pursuing, but he will knock down anyone in his way.

Although violent and often acting from instinct, he is not unaware. It is his sense of reason and balance that allows him to succeed in his wildest ambitions. He is capable and adroit but always in a hurry.

He dismisses fear as inconsequential and can act heroically, but his aim is always self-centered, never altruistic. Sometimes his lack of moral scruples gives him the power and freedom to achieve his ends in ways that the more conventional would shy away from. By nature he is incapable of experiencing remorse.

He is prey to certain vices such as drugs and alcohol and can become involved in cults. He will pass from one to another, going from drugs to alcohol or from sect to sect. It is best to be forewarned about this aspect of his character.

The presence of this card warns us that we will have to act energetically to free ourselves from a bad situation and be ready to change the status quo in order to succeed.

The Knight of Staves is a violent conqueror, swift, efficient, noble, and generous but often talkative. He is possessed of an intuitive intelligence, but one ought not rely thoroughly upon his hasty decisions. The intense energy he brings to all his enterprises can sometimes prevent him from clearly evaluating all of the contingencies involved in a situation. He sometimes expresses his opinions too forcefully. He is endowed with a fine memory, a mind that is generous, humanistic, and romantic. His devotion to justice finds expression in his constant struggle against any form of persecution of the weak. He has a passionate interest in history and tradition. His sense of humor is biting and extremely acute, his endurance extraordinary, his courage admirable. He is somewhat sensitive to outside influence, and others in certain circumstances may find it easy to manipulate him. With this knight there is an occasional risk of thievery or breaking and entering.

His presence announces that changes are going to be sudden and rapid. He suggests to us that we ought to take the time to reflect in a state of tranquillity before embarking on a course of action or making a major change in our living situation.

He can signal a change of residence or a break with old friends or relations or simply a business trip.

The Knight of Cups is a wandering lover, messenger of hidden or repressed desires and violent passions. He is intensely secretive and mysterious. This Don Juan has much experience in love. Under a calm and charming demeanor, great ambition and intensity smolder. He is endowed with artistic talent. Though his company does not promise rest or ease, it can signal a renewal, particularly in the domain of love. He also augurs secrets given in confidence or new propositions revealed.

One must be on guard not to be swept away by his impassioned romanticism and his extravagant promises of love. He has a tendency not to stick scrupulously to his given word. It is best not to trust him entirely.

Despite his many strengths and charms, one must acknowledge that there is in his character a certain lack of responsibility and will to persevere until the end is reached.

The Knight of Cups can signal an innovation or a romantic encounter or journey.

The Knight of Coins, alone among the knights, waits patiently for events to work themselves out; he does nothing to incite them. He observes the world with a detached air, moving no sooner than is absolutely necessary. Often he is somewhat soft, fond of leisure to the point of laziness.

He does not possess a refined sensibility, nor is he particularly susceptible to the appeal of the emotions. His imperturbable air often suggests a lack of concern with the thoughts of others, but this may be more apparent than real. A materialist lacking great ambition, he is nonetheless endowed with a innate sense of poise and is particularly canny in the domains of finance and business. It's a pity that he lacks drive, because even though he is slow getting started, he is to a great degree capable, organized, reflective, and methodical. A passive and rooted strength resides in him waiting to be revealed.

Often this card announces the completion of project. It can also signify a voyage or a new turn of events, both concerning financial matters.

The Pages

The page is, in principle, a man attached to the service of a house or a person. In the tarot deck this card represents either a young man or a young woman. He is complacent and discreet. He may be another's confidant, but he will guard his own opinions. Sancho Panza, that rational, proud, and eminently practical spirit, always respected the fantasies of his lord, Don Quixote: While following him into his world of folly, Sancho never lost touch with his own sense of reality.

In the middle ages there was nothing demeaning about the position of a page. The page was a young noble who trained to become a squire, to accompany the knight on his campaigns and carry his armor. This was the entry into the courtly world where he would begin his apprenticeship in arms. Eventually the young page would qualify for knighthood.

In the tarot, the page is someone in a dependent position, a child, adolescent, servant, sometimes even an animal.

The Page of Swords is a young man or woman, sometimes a child blessed with great acuity or perception. He ably evaluates the situation at hand and knows how to turn circumstances to his own advantage. He can analyze and synthesize data and is aware of danger before it is clearly manifest. He is precocious, with a brilliant and subtle intelligence. This is combined with logic, clarity, and vigilance. Like sparks, fascinating and provocative ideas flash from him, but he will rarely take the trouble to realize them. He is practical and can quickly adapt himself to changing circumstances. He can also mediate successfully between opposing parties, but he sometimes meddles in others' affairs and will perhaps spy on his neighbors.

He can be vindictive and spiteful. There is a destructive and aggressive aspect to his facility for logic. He is subject to periods of anxiety and is often found wanting in carrying out familial obligations. The family circle, in fact, is the only place in which he shows himself ill at ease.

His presence forebodes difficulty with children, accidental hurt, or perhaps betrayal by a close associate. But there is also a positive side: a favorable verdict in a lawsuit thanks to the services of an able attorney, the end of a legal problem, and sometimes a divorce by mutual consent.

The Page of Staves is a faithful and loyal friend, a benevolent emissary, a bearer of important tidings. He is a free-spirited young man, a confirmed individualist, ambitious and full of energy and enthusiasm. But in hate as well as in love he is violent, implacable. He forgets nothing and will never pardon an injury or betrayal. He evidences in all instances the quality of patience. He will wait however long is necessary to obtain his revenge. He can appear superficial, even bumptious. But beware. He is a consummate actor who knows exactly what he is doing.

He possesses wide-ranging knowledge and will go to any lengths to broaden his understanding and pursue wisdom. His goodwill is evident. Sometimes he is a

The Five Senses. Playing cards are in evidence, evoking the development of the sixth sense, which the use of the tarot confers. (S. Stoskopff, seventeenth century, Musée de l'œuvre Notre Dame, Strasbourg.)

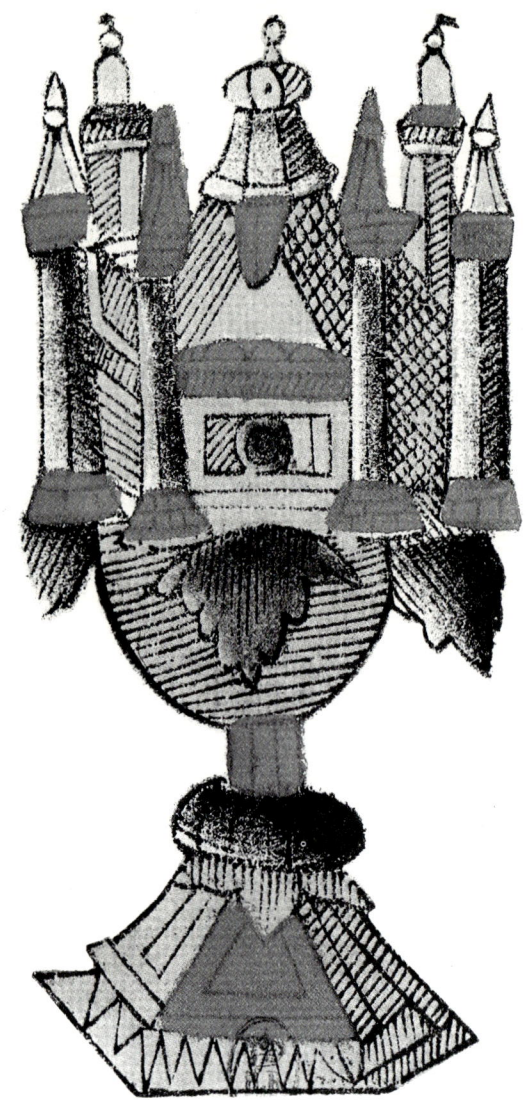

Ace of Cups (Vieville tarot) symbolizes perfect unconditional love. It represents joy, abundance, and perfection in love and friendship. It is a card of harmony and plenitude.

foreigner or temporarily in residence abroad. He can talk too much and exhibit violence in trying to force his opinions on others. Both physically and intellectually, his is a powerful and daring nature. One is immediately impressed by the force of his character.

This able and intelligent individualist carries surprising news, usually to our advantage. His message is radiant with joy and promises great things.

The Page of Cups represents a young man, or more often woman, who is gracious, friendly, and easy to get along with but lacking vitality. For this page the emotional life is of supreme importance. Studious, loyal, reflective, he is well favored, but his personality does not leave an indelible impression. He is a tender and sensual lover, but he can be somewhat incoherent in his ideas.

He deserves a certain amount of trust, but despite his good intentions his comprehension remains superficial. His character lacks structure and moral fiber; he prefers to live in a world of dream and fantasy.

At first glance, he appears egotistical and inconstant; however, he will always arrive at the end of the road that he chooses. Dependent on others, he can be an interested listener, a valuable friend, and a source of comfort and warmth. His is basically a kind nature. With this, one has to be satisfied because he is incapable of responding to the deep and hidden currents of life.

This card announces important developments in the emotional sphere; all other aspects of the personality will for a time fade into the background or hinge upon the outcome of events in this domain.

The Page of Coins is an adolescent interested in spiritual pursuits. He is a dreamer, a tender soul who never ceases to be amazed by humanity, life, and nature. His feminine temperament, has its narcissistic side but not without some justification, since he possesses inner beauty and refinement. He is motivated by a desire to learn and is fitted for meditation and study. Action for its own sake interests him not at all; he prefers to remain above day-to-day struggles.

He respects wisdom and erudition above all. Those who possess these qualities fascinate him. His perfectionism has something of the extreme about it; his faults stem from an excess of the feminine in his makeup. He can be fickle and capricious and guilty of thievery, particularly in emotional matters. Despite his love of intellectual labor, he has difficulty concentrating. He can be extravagant but always because of some spontaneously generous impulse.

This page is especially cognizant of the effect he has on those around him. He can easily change direction or alter the emphasis of his proposals to maintain harmony.

This card augurs confidences given or received or the arrival of surprising or unlooked-for news.

Numbered Minor Arcana

Everything that exists possesses a number.
It is impossible that a thing without number
be known or even imagined.

—*Philolaos (Fifth century B.C.)*

10: Message of Hope

The number 10 evokes the Wheel of Fortune of the major arcana. It reminds us that nothing is permanent

In this engraving after François Courboin (c. 1499) one can recognize one with his crown, the other with his tiara and cross, the Emperor and the Hierophant of the tarot of Marseilles, among persons apparently reflecting cards from the minor arcana. (*Revers du jeu des Suisses*: Bibliothèque nationale)

in the universe, that periods of calm will be succeeded by moments of intense activity, and that after the storm peace will reign again. Cycles of joy alternate with those of adversity, but joy will eventually return.

In the Tree of Life of the Kabbalah, this number is attributable to Malchus, the Kingdom, the culmination of all the energy in the cosmos, evolution's final end.

This card then is a message of hope and a warning that tomorrow must inevitably bring change. The number 10 represents the world in movement and a continual process of recreation.

The 10 of Swords is not a favorable card. It foretells anguish, tears, disorder, sometimes despair, dislocation, and corruption. It pertains to all that works out its destiny under cover of dark—the nocturnal life and insomnia, as well as cabals and treason. It is sometimes called the lord of ruin because it can indicate a total sacrifice of things on the material plane.

Often reason is in conflict with reality; thus the crazy logic of some philosophies. It can be a mirage that beckons us, to which we arrive haggard and lost.

Even when this card is surrounded with cards suggesting material, professional, or social success, the inner life will remain impoverished and troubled, sometimes without any apparent reason. However, all this can be a passing phase, because with the number 10, there is always an ascension and the possibility of hope. Out of the ashes one can build a new life, perhaps on a better and more lasting foundation.

The 10 of Staves indicates a change usually for the worse—it is a card that augers oppression in various

1

Valet d'Epée
The Knave of Swords

2

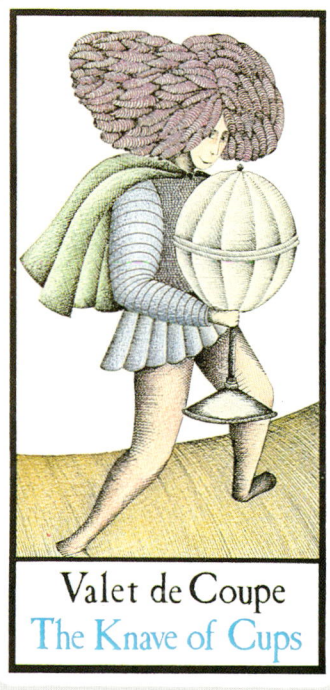

Valet de Coupe
The Knave of Cups

3

Cavalier d'Epée
The Knight of Swords

4

Reyne d'Epée
The Queen of Swords

5

Roy de Baton
The King of Clubs

6

Roy d'Epée
The King of Swords

Fourteen minor arcana from the tarot deck designed by contemporary Argentine artist Sylvia Maddoni.
1. The Page of Sword is a very young boy or girl but blessed with a remarkable perceptiveness. 2. The Page of Cups is a voluptuous sentimentalist without any coherence in his thoughts. 3. The Knight of Swords possesses a powerfully seductive nature but is egotistical and violent. 4. The Queen of Swords, secretive and distant, cherishes her independence. 5. The King of Staves is a man of influence, active and generous. He can be somewhat chauvinistic. 6. The King of Swords can with equal energy attack and defend; he is a fighter. 7. The King of Coins is a materialist; his main interests are money and worldly goods. 8. The Knight of Staves is noble hearted and generous but also violent and impulsive. 9. The Queen of Staves incarnates feminine grace and all its virtues. 10. The Knight of Cups is a thief of hearts given to artistic pursuits. 11. The Queen of Cups possesses three virtues—she is a good mother, a good wife, and a good friend. 12. The Page of Coins is tenderhearted, a dreamer, honoring learning and erudition. 13. The Queen of Coins is a married woman, rich and generous. Her sense of respectability holds her natural sensuality in check. 14. The King of Cups, often blond, is easygoing and cultivated.

Roy de Deniers
The King of Money

Cavalier de Baton
The Knight of Clubs

Reyne de Baton
The Queen of Clubs

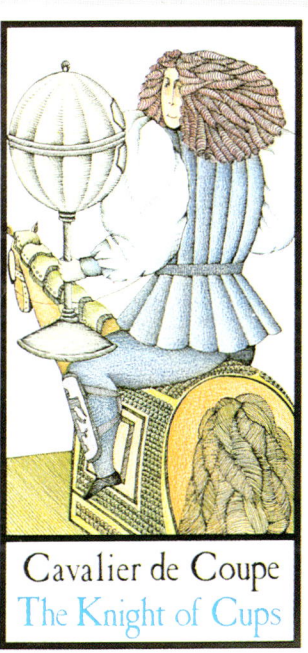

Cavalier de Coupe
The Knight of Cups

Reyne de Coupe
The Queen of Cups

Valet de Deniers
The Knave of Money

Reyne de Deniers
The Queen of Money

Roy de Coupe
The King of Cups

domains. One senses here the presence of Saturn, a planet heavy and dark. Here action is divorced from its spiritual source and becomes blind force. It is suggested that this way of acting may not be the best or only avenue of expression open to us.

Sometimes difficulty in disengaging from the influence of a parent or employer is signaled, which can stand in the way of self-realization. Often there exists the prospect of some professional, financial, or personal success, but it is to be won at great cost, and its burdens will be difficult to carry.

This card announces very intense personal pressures, overwork, exhaustion. Any power or energy available will be channeled toward strictly egotistical ends.

It introduces the idea of trouble, perfidy, opposition, obstacles that cannot be overcome, sometimes even cruelty from which it is difficult if not impossible to escape.

The 10 of Cups represents our native land but also conjugal peace, domestic harmony, sometimes a child or adolescent. It is a card of satiety but also of instability and fluctuation, influenced by Mars and uneasy under the sign of Pisces. In affairs there are sometimes difficulties to be surmounted, impediments to be cleared away. Sustained effort will prove difficult owing to fragile health. Business realized in friendly circumstances can prove profitable. With this card, one may discover a loss of interest in something that has long been wished for.

In any event, regarding all that pertains to the realm of emotions, this card is extremely beneficial. Certain esoterists call it lord of pleasure. It foretells love, perfect and shared, warm friendship, affection, tenderness, the realization of one's emotional yearnings.

The 10 of Coins signals financial independence, material success, victory in difficult enterprises, solidity, security, often an inheritance. It is named the lord of wealth. It signals great success in financial matters but also wisdom and good fortune.

If one's health is poor, the chance for recovery is high; if one is in good health, vital energies are properly channeled and put to good use. Thanks to the influence of Mercury, courage allied with presence of mind leads to great understanding. And if one stays vigilant, this prosperity will last.

In all that concerns property, this card always announces increase of one's patrimony, important and fruitful acquisitions, exceptionally profitable associations, confirmed success in all transactions.

9: Initiation

As the Hermit demonstrates, 9 is the number of passivity but also of completion. It is both beginning and end; it returns to itself and offers the prospect of regeneration. It corresponds to Yesod the Foundation, on the Tree of Life, which crystallizes and channels immense energies and is subject to the moon's influence. Zoroaster held the number 9 to be sacred and attributed it to the order of the highest perfection.

Each 9 constitutes a powerful impact of elemental focus in the material realm. Hesiod, Greek poet and sage, begins his *Theogony* (which consists of an allegorical description of the universe structured as nine celestial spheres) with an invocation to the nine Muses, one of whom, Uranie, recalls Uranus, god of heaven. It is well known that the word *music* is derived from the Muses, and Pythagoras has described at length the music of the spheres. This number then applies to the totality of man's being.

In the esoteric tradition, 9 is the number of initiation. It is replete with ritual significance. Islam emphasizes the significance of the human animal's nine orifices; these portals allow us to communicate with the world in which we have our being.

Being the last single digit, it represents, as has been pointed out, the end and the beginning of cycles and opens the way leading to transformations. It is a stepping stone leading from one plane to another. It stands for death and rebirth.

Metaphysically, it can be said to represent the return from multiplicity to the One, the ultimate reality, the Ouroboros, the worm that swallows its own tail—continuity and eternal return.

The 9 of Swords is a card of suffering, grief, and passivity in the face of adversity. It is ruled by Mars, planet of war. Here we penetrate the world of unconscious conflicts, deep-seated neuroses, and madness. Blood and poison are associated with this card.

Depending on the cards that surround it the fate that this 9 portends will relate to ill health, perhaps problems with drug addiction, or social ills, such as damaging rumor or scandal. On the level of personality, cruelty, hatred, and despair follow in its wake.

The only way to resist the evil effects of the card is to oppose it with a passive resignation in the expectation of an eventual turn for the better. Mercifully, its influence is of short duration. There is no way to avoid its power, but it will not last.

This card is the most ill omened in the minor arcana.

The 9 of Staves councils prudence, reflection, getting back to basics in our personal and working life. It can signify a journey or contact with someone from abroad. It is a card of great power and energy in the intellectual sphere, assuring us of balance between continuity and change. Change leads to regeneration; continuity provides the foundation for progress. The time is opportune; it is preferable to take action and not delay, to derive the maximum benefits from this favorable period.

Under the influence of this card, imagination is powerful and artistic creativity is released. Our work, however, must be accomplished sheltered from indiscreet companions. This card is particularly beneficial for active professions that require much movement or travel.

In general this card holds forth great opportunities in social and intellectual domains. One now finds success in relationships with others, a warm and friendly atmosphere in which understanding and the exchange of views flourish.

The 9 of Cups is by far the most favorable card in the minor arcana. It denotes perfect harmony in love and friendship. It indicates also the love of beautiful things, fine thoughts, the search for perfection. It promises complete concord between reality and our affections. Health is excellent, resistance to negative influences remarkable.

Cups correspond to water. Clearly there is some danger from illusion and fantasy—wishful thinking—considering the associations of the number 9 with the moon, which reinforces the symbolism of water. But water also suggests the idea of tranquillity and peace, sweetness and serenity.

This card refers to aesthetic as well as emotional pursuits. It is associated with the pictorial arts, painting, and decoration as well as architecture.

The 9 of Cups augurs good fortune in friendship and in love, extraordinary success, deserved recognition of merit, the most perfect joy—that happiness of which we dream.

The 9 of Coins refers to prosperity and wealth. It is especially favorable for business dealings. It signals remarkable powers of discernment, happily joined to equal powers of discretion. It does not signify the sudden or immediate attainment of wealth, but rather a gradually realized and well-deserved prosperity, due to hard work, sound investments, intelligence and foresight.

This card signals great opportunity on the material plane; it produces favorable responses from others and popularity. It promises financial security, pleasant surroundings, continuing increase—in short, unwavering progress in business and solid financial gains.

Because of the power this card portends, material and financial success is assured. It is also sometimes associated with one who loves nature, one for whom all the material advantages do not conceal its beauty.

8: Sword of Damocles

In the Tree of Life, 8 is the number of Hod, Glory. Under its influence rational intelligence imposes its limitations on the human animal. The number 8 restricts the expenditure of vital energies and controls the forces of personality. As our ability to react to situations rises above emotional reflexes to arrive at mastery and rational control, it becomes a dynamic force in our lives.

The ancients considered 8 to be the number of Pluto, god of the underworld. Because it is the first cube of a whole integer (aside from the number 1) it represents the earth, its mass and volume. It serves as a conduit between heaven and earth. Baptismal fonts, which configure rebirth into a spiritual life, of materiality's journey of self-transcendence, have eight sides.

In the minor arcana, this number often means suffering and the remorseless working out of fate. It is a sort of Damoclean sword that hangs over us and may fall at any moment. It suggests inexplicable fear, forebodings of doom, and hidden dangers. But one must be careful to base one's interpretation on the context in which it reveals itself.

It always brings in its wake a certain uneasiness, sometimes aggravated to the point of profound anxiety. However, since initiates, such as the Templars and Druids, consider it to be their governing number, its effects clearly have redeeming virtues. It can mark a change from one condition to another, and change is often accompanied by uneasiness and anxiety.

The 8 of Swords represents sadness, obstacles, discord, overwork, unexpected difficulties. It can stand for great ineluctable tragedy, a serious setback, or merely a lack of intellectual progress. The most disquieting aspect of this card speaks of repression, condemnation, imprisonment, and treason.

The 8 of Swords is sharp. It is the card of daggers, fires, and machetes. One's way is constantly being blocked by a train of accidental interferences that begin to suggest the presence of some force of actual malevolence. Health is on the wane, vital energies trickle away, weakness seizes our will. Here we face the brute force of inertia, the suspension of all activity.

We should avoid conflict, but there is a tendency to get drawn into troubles for which we are not responsible and which are difficult to define, much less resolve. Yet they are all too real and poison our existence. This

Following pages: In Joyous Company, illustration taken from a Slavic almanac (c. 1660). Here are pictured cardplayers. The deck they are using is a descendant of the tarot. One recognizes in clubs, diamonds, hearts, and spades the four suits of the tarot: staves, coins, cups, and swords.

card can forebode censure, opposition, criticism, even calumny. In any event, it brings no good news.

The 8 of Staves is the least virulent of all the 8s, although it warns us of the possibilities of quarrels and misunderstandings with those close to us. It can often suggest a certain tendency toward dispersion of energies, which can prove dangerous.

This card is impulsive, energetic, and exalted. It is particularly beneficial for physicians and mathematicians, who now have an opportunity to make great discoveries. It points toward new ideas and projects, feverish activity, success in enterprises, meetings with interesting people and the promise of rich rewards. It tells us to hasten to make decisions while the time is ripe, not to delay. A course of action embarked upon under the governance of this card will prosper, because it symbolizes creative thought harmoniously joined with exact and effective reasoning.

However, one must be on guard against impetuousness and unreasoning impulses, which can to some extent mitigate the benevolent aspects of this card. We may also be faced with the risk of isolation, a lack of communication with our fellows.

The 8 of Cups signifies sadness and disillusionment, the loss of an ideal, the fall from a world of dreams into one of bitterness.

This card, ruled by water, does not refer to the sea, but rather to lagoons, to deep, stagnant waters, to mud pools and fens. These polluted waters are breeding grounds for germs, miasmas, and hidden poisons.

There is a complete loss of interest in life, the aban-

The depiction of a tarot reader of the middle ages is totally anachronistic, because at this period tarot cards were not in use in Europe. They did not come into circulation until after the invention of printing. (Engraving dated 1840; Bibliothèque des arts decoratifs.)

donment of projects undertaken, indolence, hesitation, a sort of paralysis of the will. Now and then this card announces the arrival of a long-awaited event. More often, it signals problems in marital relations, perhaps caused by sadness or depression on the part of one partner, or perhaps simply estrangement and distance between friends.

It is impossible to react sanely under these conditions. This card signifies deception, loss of self, profound and enervating nostalgia, sometimes an infinite sadness for reasons that remain quite inexplicable.

The 8 of Coins counsels prudence and the preservation of present financial security and the serenity we have obtained in the arena of our emotions. It is useful, nay indispensable, not to act for the moment, but rather to wait to see what events will bring. What is at stake is not difficult to comprehend, for this card applies strictly to the material realm.

This card can describe a situation in which circumstances are sufficiently happy and calm. We ought not overstep our bounds, but rather be content with what we have. We have here a pleasant union, shared love, modest and tranquil, devoid of passion and stormy emotions. Life unfolds in an atmosphere of calm; sentiment is restrained, and the spirit of adventure holds no appeal. There is perhaps little emotional investment on the part of either partner.

This card can also suggest the entering into apprenticeship or definite manual skills, particularly in the fields of agriculture and mechanics. It can also signify the birth of a child.

7: The Holy Number

Seven is the number victory and harmony. The law of 7 governs all creation. 7 manifests the cosmic order, the organization of universal energies. To be in "seventh heaven" is to find supreme felicity. 7 represents the perfect dynamic of cyclical completion and renewal. This cosmic number is held to be sacred by almost all religions. The Bible and the Qur'an are filled with sets of sevens.

This number encompasses the totality of moral life, combining the three theological virtues with the four cardinal virtues. In discussing its potency, Hippocrates described it in the following terms: "The number 7, through its hidden virtues, sustains the being of all created things; it dispenses life and movement, even the celestial spheres feel its influence." It is endowed with magical and mythic properties and initiates vast transformations.

However an uncontrollable anxiety accompanies its

The Ace of Staves (Besancon tarot) is a virile and intellectual card, strongly marked with the spirit of enterprise, personal initiative, and creativity in work. It ushers in a very favorable time out of which we can expect great practical benefits, sometimes including great wealth.

effects, implying as it does the passage from the known into the unknown. Transformation must usher in the beginning of a new cycle, and anxiety follows change, especially in the face of the mysterious uncertainty of new life.

In the tarot deck, the 7 stirs up some conflict. Comfort and security reveal themselves to be unstable. They cannot be taken for granted. To preserve them, one must take active steps. If one applies oneself, the prospects for success are good.

The 7 of Swords offers hope when our affairs are going badly. One must not depend upon good fortune, but rather on our own continuing efforts. We can reach our goal. It tells us to listen to good counsel, to persevere with confidence and courage, and to pursue our aims

The great deck of Bellini spells out the signification of all the arcana.
Even those unfamiliar with the symbolism of the tarot can use them.
These cards can be read right-side-up or upside-down, giving rise
to different interpretations. They were conceived and drawn by a

celebrated clairvoyant of the nineteenth century, Edmond, disciple of Mademoiselle Lenormand. Bellini, also a psychic, rediscovered them by an extraordinary stroke of luck and had them reproduced.

with unwavering dedication. Our fate is in our own hands.

There is some degree of debate, disagreement, and vain disputation, but our will prevails in the long run as long as we defend our position with courage and clarity.

This card often brings tidings of a long-sought-for union. If it is ill aspected, there may be delays and obstacles to overcome, but in the end it will take place. The card has nothing to do with chance. We can be sure that the rewards we reap are due solely to our own hard work.

Occasionally this card notifies us to be on guard against theft. Most of the time, however, the 7 of Swords encourages us to channel our energies and force toward the completion of our goals.

It is good to know with certitude that if we are willing to work for it, we can obtain what we desire.

The 7 of Staves announces great material success, accomplishment in our professional endeavors, and sometimes good fortune in lotteries or games of chance. Its influence is dynamic and invigorating. Victories that seemed most in doubt or difficult to obtain suddenly fall into our laps, and the strongest and most stubborn enemies are overcome with little apparent effort. Discussions and negotiations are sure to lead to positive results.

It is absolutely necessary to profit from this favorable climate for action and energetically pursue our aims before the vital forces disperse. One must above all have courage—the courage of our convictions, the courage to act and succeed.

It is likely that one will develop an excellent relationship with a co-worker of the other sex. Sportsmen and adventurers should not delay their projects even for an instant. This is the propitious moment, but it will not last forever.

The 7 of Cups pertains exclusively to the affective life. Here one must exercise great self-control. One finds with this card an overmastering attraction to drugs, strong drink, debilitating pleasures, and a manner of living so undisciplined and irregular that it can disrupt one's mental and physical equilibrium. Surrounded by unfavorable influences, the card can refer to frenzied debaucheries. One must distrust one's own whims and inclinations.

A more positive aspect of this card suggests transcendence of selfish impulses in love, altruism to the extent of complete giving of self. It can be a matter of a very tender friendship, secret love, or simply a great love of beauty. Beware of certain illusory signs of success, for there is a definite risk of succumbing to wishful thinking.

The 7 of Cups also indicates an active and fertile imagination. This can be frittered away in dreams and fantasies, but on the other hand, if we exercise control and channel it properly it can lead to great artistic and creative achievements.

The 7 of Coins does not refer to emotions or good health. It announces an influx of hard cash. This, the result of long and careful efforts, does not depend on external forces. It is culmination we have sought, the achievement of our financial goals thanks to daily work and wise husbandry of resources.

This card also bodes good fortune to those in the arts. Now they can see realized what before had been a work of their imagination. For those who carefully planted the seed and diligently tended it, the harvest is now at hand.

In short, the 7 of Coins represents the actualization on the material plane of a creation that was conceived with difficulty, and this emergence of the idea into reality has a guarantee of success.

6: Fluctuation and Hesitation

In the *Sepher Yetzirah*, 6 is the number of Tiphares, seated at the center of the Kabbalic Tree of Life; it is at the crossroads of the pathways of wisdom. Tiphares lies on the central column of the tree, the trunk that supports consciousness. In Hebrew, Tiphares signifies Beauty. True beauty consists in the relationship of harmonious forms, on the material as on the moral and spiritual planes. This Sephirah is also entitled the Sphere of the Sun. It occupies the same centrality on the tree as the sun does in our solar system. Similarly the solar plexus is one of the most important centers of energy in the human being. Tiphares represents in the microcosm superior psychic force and consciousness of self. A strong sense of self is indispensable, but this attitude has the potential for narcissism, which can impede us from joining with others. This Sephirah emphasizes the centrality of self but simultaneously points out the necessity of communion with those around us for a fulfilled life.

In the tarot the number 6 represents above all hesitation, difficulties that can be smoothed over or deflected, and opposition that one can shape for good. It can, however, also signify a change for the worse, uprisings, and revolt. In some instances, the effects of this revolt are not fully felt and manifest themselves under the guise of nostalgic longings or feelings of frustration. It's not wise to do battle with these rather slippery and melancholy impressions, because 6 is inherently changeable, sensitive to its surroundings, rarely evil in its effects, and often a positive force.

The 6 of Cups announces an irresistible nostalgia combined with a pronounced desire for change. Happily, its pessimistic atmosphere is fleeting, because we have a strong disposition for happiness. We must cast away negative and debilitating thoughts and cultivate our capacity for altruism.

(*Lower left*) Two cards from the Visconti-Sforza deck. The 6 of Staves balances our energies, although sometimes it can hold forth promise of a victory that is not really within our grasp. However, if we are patient and await the right moment to act, we will realize our desires all the same. Success will be manifested on the personal rather than the material plane.

The 6 of Swords brings with it rewards for those who have worked steadily toward a goal. It is particularly applicable to business affairs but can also refer to emotional attachments. Clouds disperse, and well-deserved success appears over the horizon and rapidly advances toward us. There may be some persisting difficulties, but these will be shaken off with little effort. Intelligent action will ensure success.

A voyage abroad can help us gain advancement in business after a period of doubt and anxiety.

For scientists, this card is especially favorable. It can mean an important discovery, one with potentially wide-ranging beneficial effects.

For the suffering and sick a remedy is near.

The success at hand, whether financial or emotional, is richly deserved. It comes about because of the exercise of our intelligence and our understanding of and empathy for others.

The 6 of Staves balances our energies, although sometimes it can hold forth promise of a victory which is not really in our grasp. If we are patient and await the right moment to act, we will realize our desires all the same. Success will be accomplished on the personal rather than the material plane.

Surrounded by other positive cards, the 6 brings victory, harmony, and beauty. In the company of less benign influences, there is the possibility of doubt and hesitation—what once seemed certain may now be called into question. Depression can easily proceed from a premature optimism.

We must nonetheless trust in and hope for a success that has less to do with property, money, or love than psychological progress. Now is a time for the cultivation of self, mastery of our weaknesses, striking a proper balance between the inner and the outer man. The 6 of staves then is card of the regeneration of our interior life.

The 6 of Cups combines an indisputable sense of nostalgia with a pronounced desire for change. We sink into reverie. Memories of the past take hold of our spirits and can plunge us into a profound melancholy. It is as if we drown in a few inches of water. Trifles take on deep and inexplicable resonances. There are in evidence certain health problems and a distinct lowering of vital energies. This trouble will, however, be fleeting because our capacity for health and happiness endures, veiled for the time being by this darkened atmosphere.

We can take refuge in our own recuperative powers and rely on the natural healing energy that is always present within us. It is no time to abandon oneself to sick fancies. On the contrary, we must reject the destructive thoughts that assail us.

Now is a good time to bring into play our capacity for selfless love. This will pave the way for a full enjoyment of the good things that life offers and aid the process of self-unfolding.

The 6 of Coins responds with a resounding *Yes* to the question posed it. Under its influence, we witness equilibrium of forces, harmony in our immediate circle, and successful cooperation in our work. Business and personal relations will be founded on reciprocal intent and understanding.

Health is good; physical resistance at its height. Happiness seems permanently installed, material well-being ensured. The union between two persons is perfected; each feels at home with the other. Our thoughts are wide ranging, affectionate, and compassionate.

The individual seems to vibrate in harmony with the world around him. This wonderful feeling is serene and exalted at the same time. There is also a possibility of an unlooked-for gift or legacy.

This card is so powerfully benign that it attenuates the effects of the cards surrounding it, all the more if they are considered to be especially ill omened.

5: Warlike Virtues

In the Kabbalah 5 is attributed to Gevurah, Strength. This is the most dynamic but also the most violent of the Sephiroth. It is, however, extremely disciplined. 5 corresponds to Mars, the god of war, who imposes a discipline equal to his strength. Energy and courage are his virtues; cruelty and destruction his negative aspects. Under no circumstances does Gevurah represent the enemy; it is always the knight who sets out to war to battle injustice.

5, then, indicates power, domination, victory in all sorts of battles and conflicts. It is the number of human manifestation, of material and empirical existence. It has its calibrating and mediating aspects, but these are always evidenced in action. 5 represents the action of the mind and personality on the world.

There is a surplus of energy. This can be directed toward useful and constructive enterprises, but to wanton acts of destruction as well. One can mount to heaven or descend to hell. It is never calm or passive but always active, forceful, and violent.

Nietzschean in some of its ramifications, the number 5 considers mercy, tenderness, and love to be virtues of the slave. Its ideal is glory in combat, great deeds, courage, justice, and strength.

The 5 of Swords is a card of conflicting impulses.

There is much friction and struggle. Victory can quickly turn into defeat due to the intense exhaustion of our forces. Feelings blind intelligence, and intelligence is out of touch with its emotional bases.

In love, we can find ourselves faced with an impasse or an actual defeat, because of our inability to capitalize on progress made, whether on account of pride, profound neglect, or inertia. We are too concerned with what others think of us, put too much stock in external appearances, and this blocks our progress.

We must guard against corruption, aggressiveness, and trickery and be careful not to harm others. We can do great damage in our unthinking efforts to extricate ourselves from the conflicts in which we are embroiled. This is a violent and warlike card, and it carries the risk suffering defeat owing to poor organization.

The 5 of Staves indicates conflict in all aspects of life and willfulness to the point of perfect obstinacy. One is in full possession of one's faculties but a gnawing dissatisfaction poisons all endeavors.

One must fight against pride and stubbornness and learn how to listen to the good advice of others. This card often indicates a most unpleasant kind of overbearing and dominating personality. A more tractable demeanor can prove very beneficial. In the company of cards with negative influences, the 5 of Staves warns us of unending conflicts and disputes and sometimes a loss of employment, due to difficulties in adapting to others and a self-defeating intolerance. We should guard against anger.

However, thanks to the volcanic energy that the number 5 represents, there exists a good chance of success

The Fortune Teller. This engraving, taken from the periodical *Le Bon Genre* (c. 1800), is accompanied by a sagacious comment: "She made their credulity her science." Then as now cartomancy is too often practiced by charlatans. (Bibliothèque des arts decoratifs.)

and enrichment, especially if we seize the proper moment to act. Willingness to throw ourselves into battle and perseverance in our efforts can lead to extremely positive results.

The 5 of Cups is a card of tension and conflict on the emotional plane. Our desires are exacerbated, our passions dark and violent.

We ignore good counsel and find ourselves prey to a debilitating and oppressive anxiety. Frustration rules the day. Matter triumphs over spirit.

The energy we have at our disposal is considerable, but it is badly channeled and intermittent; consequently, the quality of our work is uneven and, over the long run, deteriorates. In any case, we will not be able to avoid some injury. Sometimes this card announces an inheritance, but the material benefit cannot make up for the emotional loss involved.

In the wake of this card come domination of others, deception in love, and disappointment in friendship.

The 5 of Coins is the lover. Here arise the dangers provoked by love outside the bounds of marriage. There is no question of calm and tender affection sanctioned by law and the community; on the contrary, here is overweening tension and passion that transgress social bounds.

Often this card announces material or financial setbacks that can be literally ruinous in their effects. It also can indicate tormenting anxieties, even obsession.

This card also refers to violent and explosive unleashing of terrestrial forces, natural catastrophes such as earthquakes, storms, and tornadoes. It refers to social turmoil as well—strikes, riots, disorders of all sorts, war, and revolution

With this card the qualities of the heart are missing: There exists passion but not tenderness or affection.

4: Solidity, Passivity.

Kabbalists assign the number 4 to Chesed, Kindness, on the Tree of the Sephiroth. It evokes a majestic king, seated on his throne (see the Emperor in the major arcana), who organizes the direction and resources of his kingdom. The warrior king of the fifth Sephirah has descended from his chariot and sets about establishing law and bringing order to the land. Fully aware of earthly duties, he looks beyond the material plane and elevates his consciousness. Mars is displaced by Jupiter, protector and benevolent ruler.

The primary virtue associated with the number 4 is obedience. We must sacrifice some of our own independence for the sake of the commonweal. Intelligence becomes receptive; it synthesizes and concretizes the abstract.

With 4 comes the harvest. It is the number of earth, physical elements, materiality. It can indicate blockages, obstacles that stand in the way of our deepest longings. It governs the solid and tangible, all that can be felt and touched. It is the manifest universe.

This is the number of the square and the cross. It unites in man two principles, the horizontal and the vertical. One allows man to reach for the stars, the other to dwell productively in the incarnate world of flesh and human sentiments.

The number 4 is solid and structured but perfectly passive. It does not act.

The 4 of Swords announces a time of repose that succeeds a period of sustained struggle or conflict. It can be a matter of retreat, of leaving those close to us, of deception in romance, or of a disenchantment that may require sweeping changes in our day-to-day life.

This card often denotes a rigid personality, a career soldier, or a judge. It possesses a dogmatic character, erects barriers, closes doors, creates distance between people. It ushers in a period of solitude, perhaps an imposed exile, though this will not be of long duration. It can indicate jealousy on the part of someone close to us or economic difficulties. Beware of avarice. Badly aspected, it can signal war or social upheavals.

One must now take advantage of the quiet time that this card offers, this respite in the daily grind of existence, to restore one's vital energies and attain the serenity necessary for future creativity and new enterprises.

The 4 of Staves indicates that there is a benevolent and protective force at work in our affairs: It counsels us that the time is ripe to embark on long-term projects and that we can take decisive action at the right moment. Despite unavoidable difficulties, we will attain the goal we seek.

Numerous developments are occurring that are going to have a most salutary effect on our plans, but they are not of our doing; in fact, we probably will not even know what they are. Though unconscious of the fact, we are surrounded by beneficial influences. New undertakings will be concluded and put on a firm footing in the near future.

In emotional matters, although there exists the probability of some quarrels and dissensions, the protective power of this card will keep us from any serious missteps. There is in fact an equally strong likelihood of our forming an important emotional bond.

The Card Players. The deck of playing cards has twelve face cards, which bring to mind the signs of the zodiac, and the joker, which is directly derived from the Fool of the major arcana. (L. Van Leyden, c. 1520, National Gallery, Washington, D.C.)

The 3 of Coins announces well-deserved recompense for our efforts. This illustration carries the motto of the Visconti-Sforza family: "A bon droyt."

The 4 of Cups signifies a desperate search for pleasure at the expense of all other values. One is totally enslaved to the senses. There is a real danger that ephemeral passions will have a lasting destructive impact. The strength of these desires, the mental disorder that follows in their wake, can lead to bitter experiences, painful delusions, and loss of love.

Love is identified exclusively with physical pleasure. All is immersed in sensuality. Although it is possible to aspire to something purer and higher, it is difficult if not impossible to arrive at it.

For this reason there is a tendency to seek refuge in superficial and insubstantial forms of happiness. These will of course prove to be fleeting and frustrating and will eventually lead to a weakening of moral fiber and a dependency on luxury. This in turn gives rise to profound disgust and self-loathing. In any event this is a stagnant period in life, one in which we seem to be carried along by thoughts that are beyond our control.

The 4 of Coins promises power without aggression and maintains order with reason. Reason is its dominant characteristic. Less favorable are its compulsive aspects. The 4 of Coins insists on keeping everything in its proper place. Romantic attachments can suffer from frequent separations or arguments. Though there will not be violent disagreements or the danger of divorce, there persists a tiring succession of petty grievances, deliberate misunderstandings, and hurtful words uttered without any care for the other's feelings. Minor storms assail our daily life.

Love of money and desire for financial security can lead to unattractive hoarding of possessions. This can be a further step on a road leading to avarice, miserliness, and ultimately a total refusal to share any of our substance even with our immediate family.

This card sometimes presages an unexpected gift. Near a card associated with pregnancy, it foretells the birth of a daughter.

3: Creation and Dynamism

3 stands for the holy trinity. It is birth, life, and death; youth, adulthood, and old age; past present, and future. 3 signifies rivalry overcome—synthesis, reunion, and equilibrium. It is exemplified by the child, who in effect unites the mother and the father. Pythagoreans affirmed that the triangle is the principle of the generation of all created things and structures the form of manifestation. It applies also to the hierarchy of human pursuits—material, rational, and spiritual—and to the phases of the mystic's path—detachment, illumination, unity.

3 is attributed to Binah, Intelligence, Comprehension, on the Tree of Life. It represents the feminine principle's creative power in the universe. In the major arcana it is the Empress, who creates the form in which life manifests itself, the Great Mother. It governs death as well as birth, since all created things are born to die. Life animates matter, then escapes transformed. Binah

also finds expression in the personage of Kali, Hindu goddess of destructive forces. The triangle, a symbol of Saturn in his role of god of materiality, is used in magical rites to invoke a spiritual presence in the material world. 3 is a creative and active numeral, which symbolizes dynamism and manifestation on the material plane.

With the 3 of Swords we enter a world of dolorous and painful thoughts. On the emotional plane it forebodes troubles with children, family quarrels, exhaustion, and sexual frustration.

The 3 of Swords is the only 3 in the arcana that has not gone beyond rivalry to overcome duality.

On the material plane, work does not succeed in fulfilling our aspirations. Misunderstanding reigns between collaborators. There exists a kind of sourness, product of opposition, of canceled projects and disappointment.

There is a definite risk of ill health or physical harm. Even if this card is well aspected, it is best to remain vigilant. It calls to mind the Marian symbolism of the heart pierced with a sword. It is a card of trial, adversity, and sorrow. One feels misunderstood and unloved.

This card can signal a rupture or separation. On the material plane absence or delay, a large cash outlay, also a move or voluntary departure can be expected.

The 3 of Staves is powerful in the domain of creativity. It represents dynamic and well-established energy. It supports numerous projects and dispenses a salutary energy that asks only to be manifested. It excels in personal initiatives that have a solitary or individualistic character.

An entrepreneurial spirit in business aided with foresight allows us to realize commercial ventures and brings about original ideas that will enable us to smooth over any difficulties that may present themselves.

Now is not a time for procrastination. We ought to set to work with optimism and with our eyes firmly fixed upon our goal. Because our attitude is based on

The 3 of Swords (Vieville deck) cautions us to be extremely vigilant: It portends malady, adversity, and sorrow.

On the other hand, the 3 of Cups (Vieville deck) foretells that frustration will vanish, to be replaced with good fortune and good cheer.

sane and realistic perceptions, good things are bound to come our way.

Next to a card signifying a journey, this presages excellent results from travel.

The 3 of Cups is extremely beneficial in all things to do with our emotions. It announces a favorable and lasting intervention, great reward for past pains. It seems to possess some magical protective force: Happiness has been won. One is surrounded by good friends, good counsel, and good cheer.

This guiding star ushers in the return of happiness, the end of uncertainty, the solution to troubling problems. There is a very good chance of obtaining the healing for which we have been looking for so long.

This card signifies comfort and abundance in all areas of life.

Friendship, warm and sheltering, yields great joy. All our relations are harmonious. This then is a card of great good fortune. It can announce the creation of a new enterprise, the launching of a happy relationship, the birth of a child.

The 3 of Coins announces progress in our working life. The card disperses its energy to enable us to acquire financial independence, thanks to skill in commerce. It also promises success in artistic endeavors.

Mastery and accomplishment in our chosen field, or notable artistic talent, lead by their very nature to success, even celebrity. Our rewards will be twofold—financial recompense but also renown and a position of influence. It is essential not to let this extremely favorable time slip away. Take advantage of the abundant creative energy that is now present. In the near future success, even glory, will come our way.

In the personal arena this is bound to be a time of great progress, in large part because of the nobility of our aspirations and a certain breadth of character and spirit. It is a time to realize the best in ourselves.

2: Dialogue or Contradiction

This number corresponds to Chochmah, Wisdom, the second Sephirah in the Kabbalah. Here we have male energy, dynamic, constructive, stimulating evolution and change. 2 is life in its original stage of manifestation. Chochmah parallels the lingam of Hinduism, the phallus of the Greeks, not in its sexual aspect, but rather in the sense of vital dynamic force.

All phases of evolution begin with a chaotic instability that is transformed bit by bit into an organized mode of existence founded on a dynamic equilibrium. 2 is of course absolute duality. Consequently, it is the origin of the devil and all that he engenders. It is the revolt against unity, the beginning of multiplicity, opposition as well as reflection and ambivalence.

It can signify equilibrium brought about by evolution or imbalance caused by latent conflicts. Here we see rivalry, which can end in hatred and strife, but also reciprocity, which is the foundation of all fruitful relationships.

2 is dialogue and contradiction. Without ugliness we cannot know beauty. Good is perceived and understood only in relation to evil, and one knows oneself only in relation to others. 2 is I and thou. If man exists as a thinking animal, it is because he compares and makes distinctions.

The 2 of Swords designates a state of superficial inertia combined with profound internal turmoil. This card speaks of severe conflicts, which cannot break to the surface. We cannot find the means to express them. It is the calm that comes right before the storm. Its equilibrium is highly unstable. At any moment it can be overwhelmed by powerful unresolved tensions. This card also speaks of an adversary or a hidden enemy.

It is a time of truce, not peace. But we must seize this fleeting moment of respite to gather up our forces before returning to do battle. It is like the few seconds in a boxing match during which each fighter goes to his corner to regroup. Often the battle is an interior one, referring to psychological conflicts that are now making themselves felt.

As applied to matters of health this card predicts a temporary remission but not a complete cure. There is, however, a real improvement in one's condition.

In matters of love, complications can be resolved if both partners can agree to work together with willingness and clarity.

The 2 of Staves is a source of imbalance. It gives rise to doubt and dissatisfaction. But destruction is often the first step toward creation or reconstruction. There is present in this card an active and incisive element, doubt and anxiety. If one can master its contradictory impulses, they can be turned toward the good and produce lasting beneficial effects.

The 2 of Staves announces the meeting of two personalities who will either connect or rub each other the wrong way, depending on the cards that surround it. If it is above a favorable card it suggests that success, particularly on the material plane, is likely, but it will not be achieved by the most scrupulous methods.

At work there exist courage and boldness, but we will not be able to avoid confrontations with partners over ideas and methods.

1. The 2 of Swords (Visconti-Sforza deck) is a card of conflict, of heightened tension that cannot find an outlet. Peace is external, wholly provisional; open war may break out at any minute.

2. The 2 of Staves (Rider-Waite deck) engenders doubt and anxiety; however, success is likely, though it may not be attained in the easiest or most direct fashion.

3. The 2 of Coins (Besançon deck) means a change for the better, a new departure based on a more solid foundation, and a fruitful partnership in our chosen field.

Ten cards from a deck based on the I Ching. The I Ching, or Book of Changes, is one of the oldest Chinese books. Tradition attributes to the emperor Fu-Hsi, who lived 5,800 years ago, the invention of the eight trigrams whose combinations give birth to 64 hexagrams. Lao-tzu and Confucius both spent long years meditating on these. These Chinese sages affirmed that the I Ching is a luminous path that teaches us to read the order of the universe. Consciousness of the laws that govern our lives, which is the fruit of profound medita-

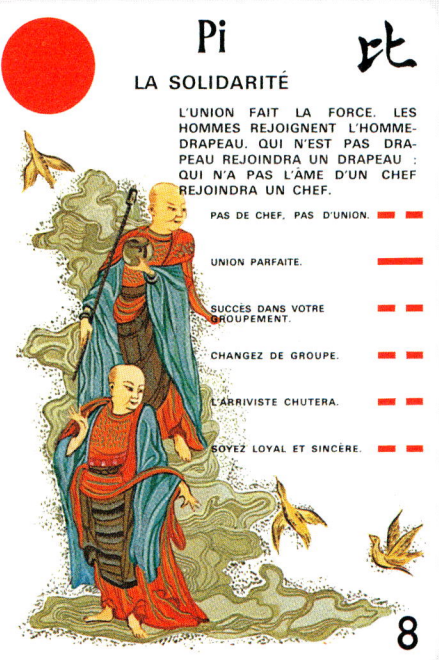

tion, allows us to look into the future and so moderate our conduct to bring about the most favorable results. This is the connection between the I Ching and the tarot. This book was unknown in Europe until it was brought back by Jesuits who had done missionary work in China in the seventeenth century. Magisterially translated by Richard Wilhelm, a missionary who lived in China, this book fascinated Carl Jung.

The 2 of Cups indicates the duality of love or friendship. Whether on a physical, emotional, or spiritual plane, there is bound to be confrontation, but this does not necessarily have to be destructive. It can refer to organized debates, philosophical discussions, or amorous tension; all these have constructive possibilities. Perfect agreement can lead to stagnation or the chance of losing one's own voice and individuality. There will exist the temptation to adopt the views and characteristics of one's partner.

With this card look for new friendships or the renewal of an old one. It announces engagements, weddings, or simply the beginning of a cooperative venture. In any event, this is a time for uniting with another whether for reasons of love or simply out of mutual self-interest.

No matter what part of our life is involved here, it is best to guard our independence to avoid being subsumed by the plans and desires of another, to remain free in one's own thoughts and actions.

The 2 of Coins signifies a happy change. A highly

The Ace of Coins from the Vieville deck enumerates in old French some of the major arcana. The Templars cross is found in the center.

The Ace of Staves (Rider-Waite deck) pertains to the world of the mind and the creative impact of intelligence. Here emotion has no place.

placed and influential person, who nonetheless lives very simply, will bring about an unlooked-for improvement in our situation. This change will have long-lasting positive effects. It is a modulation of polarized forms that establishes equilibrium at a more developed level.

This card indicates a new departure based on more solid foundations or a business association that will help us through present difficulties. One should be prudent where financial matters are concerned and avoid contracting debts that may be difficult to repay. One should also watch for a possible administrative foulup, but even if this does occur the consequences should not be too serious.

In certain instances this card reveals the presence of literary gifts that ought to be cultivated.

1—The Ace: Absolute Consciousness

The aces are not elements in themselves, but rather seeds that contain within themselves the promise of germination. They are attributed to Kesser, the Crown of the Tree of Life, primordial being, the depths of origination. This Sephirah represents the unity that underlies and exists prior to polarity. It is formless possibility, but distinct from En Soph, nonbeing, as discussed in the Kabbalah. Here we have the beginning and the culmination of the Great Work.

The ace is charged with powerful and fecund energy. It is the creative principle of the universe. We should recall that the actual sense of the word *universe* is "turned toward the one." Pascal spoke of the universe as an all-embracing unity. Regarding a passage from Empedocles, Teilhard de Chardin evokes in *Mon Universe* the divine unity from which issues multiplicity:

> "All occurs as if the One is formed by a continuous unifying of the many, and as if it were all the more perfect in that it brings together ever more perfectly an ever expanding multiplicity."

The ace, then, has supreme creative value. It is the card of pure and perfect intelligence, of synthesis, arrival, absolute consciousness.

The Ace of Swords represents the primordial energy of air. It disperses the clouds that can darken our spirits and dull our mental processes. It brooks no evasion. Intelligence is remarkable, but it does not forgive errors. Its force dominates, cuts right to the heart of the matter. It wants to conquer, not create consensus, to possess but not love. Sexuality is violent, exigent, irresistible. It neither wants nor is able to wait.

This is the card of power, conquest, total domination. It permits neither rivals nor contradiction. It commands and requires obedience.

Sometimes this card announces public ceremonies, official functions, political and civic obligations.

The powerful force of this card can cause problems if it is not channeled in accordance with our ideals. It represents savage, untamed force. This energy can lead to audacious enterprises. Under its influence we can accomplish the impossible, but it can also signify brutality and tyranny.

The Ace of Staves refers to the written word, to intellectual activity, to cultivation of the mind. It deals with the world of thought, with scholars and learned discourse. The time is propitious for creative work; the ace looses inventive and creative powers.

It is also a card of realization and adventure. It represents the head and all that relates to it on the physical as well as the intellectual plane.

This card has nothing to do with emotions; it is strictly cerebral. It presages unlooked-for gains, the beginning of new enterprises, an inheritance, or perhaps a birth.

It can indicate that we are about to embark on a decisive experience, where action and thought are unified. This intelligence descends from the abstract to realize itself in creation.

The Ace of Cups has the form of the Grail, the symbol of perfection that was so long and ardently sought by the Knights of the Round Table. The ace, along with Grail, is a representation of the heart, considered both as physical organ and ruler of our emotions.

The Ace of Swords (Visconti-Sforza deck) is a card of conquest, of power and domination, even of tyranny. Here the head conceals the heart. It knows no obstacle, no delay.

This card points to that absolute love that sustains heart and soul, the warmth of hearth, home, and family. This warmth of feeling is everywhere in evidence. There are joy, opulence, pleasure, plenitude, perfection in love and friendship. Desire exists, but healthy desire; passion also, but a passion far removed from the destructive madness represented by some other cards. The ace stands for beauty and harmony, artistic talents and supreme felicity in love.

The ace relates to our emotional nature and guarantees fruitful relationships and understanding between people. It is a sweet and loving intelligence, the intelligence of the heart.

The Ace of Coins is an exceedingly favorable card. It celebrates material prosperity and spiritual well-being. It acts on both planes. It has the capacity to erase the evil effects of surrounding cards of ill omen and heighten the benefits to be expected from favorable ones.

It is triumph in the material world, perfect luck, success in all our comings and goings. It is achievement, prosperity, the realization of ambitions, beatitudes.

It is also the card of fabulous riches. It refers to treasures, art collections, gold, and coins. It concerns, as well, the sense of precision, competence, financial genius. Here is embodied practical intelligence.

How to Read the Minor Arcana

The dominant suit gives us a very important preliminary indication of the direction of a particular reading. If there are approximately equal numbers of each suit, the near future will in all likelihood consist of setbacks and struggles but also creative endeavors that will reap financial rewards. This lucrative but difficult period will be eased by affection and warmth in our emotional affairs. When swords predominate, they announce sig-

---

KING OF STAVES—10 OF STAVES . . . Opposition

QUEEN OF SWORDS—9 OF SWORDS . . . Loneliness

KNIGHT OF SWORDS—7 OF SWORDS . . . Revolt

KNIGHT OF COINS—5 OF COINS . . . To fight for one's ideals

ANY KNIGHT—4 OF CUPS . . . Unrestrained sexuality

ANY KNIGHT—5 OF CUPS . . . Thwarted sexuality

PAGE OF SWORDS—8 OF COINS . . . Difficulties with children

10 OF SWORDS—4 OF CUPS . . . Nights of passion

10 OF SWORDS—9 OF STAVES . . . Insomnia

10 OF COINS—8 OF STAVES . . . Financial uncertainties and fluctuations

ANY STAVE—10 OF STAVES . . . A voyage

9 OF SWORDS—8 OF SWORDS . . . A significant obstacle

9 OF SWORDS—7 OF SWORDS . . . Depression

9 OF COINS—AN ILL-FAVORED STAVE . . . Infidelity

9 OF COINS—AN ILL-FAVORED SWORD . . . Poor health

8 OF STAVES—9 OF COINS . . . Fruitless initiatives

7 OF COINS—9 OF STAVES . . . Coldness, indifference

5 OF STAVES—ANY ACE . . . Good counsel that we ought follow

5 OF STAVES—5 OF SWORDS . . . Loss of employment

5 OF STAVES—5 OF CUPS . . . Beware of pride

5 OF STAVES—4 OF STAVES . . . Victory in battle

5 OF COINS—4 OF STAVES . . . Victory in battle

4 OF COINS—4 OF STAVES . . . Material success

4 OF CUPS—5 OF CUPS . . . Coldness, sterility

4 OF CUPS—5 OF SWORDS . . . Depression

4 OF CUPS—ANY CARD INDICATING PREGNANCY . . . Birth of a boy

4 OF COINS—ANY CARD INDICATING PREGNANCY . . . Birth of a girl

2 OF STAVES—4 OR 5 OF CUPS . . . Joy that will not last

2 OF STAVES—6 OF CUPS . . . Fragile happiness

2 OF STAVES—7 OF SWORDS . . . Sterile discussion

ACE OF STAVES—ANY CUP . . . Trust, the beginning of a friendship

ACE OF STAVES—ANY SWORD . . . A struggle to preserve what has been won

ACE OF CUPS—ANY STAVE . . . Difficulties with relationships

ACE OF CUPS—ANY SWORD . . . A struggle to maintain one's balance

nificant conflicts and numerous difficulties, but they also offer the possibility of creating the constructive solutions that can arise from an adversarial relationship. Staves govern action and movement, spontaneous and determined creativity. Cups disclose actions and changes in our emotional lives, in all that concerns love and friendship. Coins refer to material conditions, depicting our financial situation and what we may hope to receive insofar as money and property are concerned.

Swords and staves together foretell great activity: Though shot through with conflicting tendencies, they can be very fruitful in creative and artistic domains. Swords and cups oppose each other; it is very difficult to harmonize them. Swords and coins signal material setbacks; we will have to face somewhat straitened financial circumstances. Staves and cups combine inspiration to the creative energy that flows from it. Staves and coins incite us to travel, with the object of gaining the wealth that is due us. Cups and coins do not favor action but presage peace, harmony, and good fortune.

The list on the facing page is by its very nature incomplete, but the student should quickly be able to pick up a sense of ther associations. When in doubt, place a third card on top of the first two. This should yield further insight into the proper interpretation of their relationship. With a little practice, one becomes aware of certain clear and unambiguous correspondences between cards.

Who originally brought the Tarot into Europe? Tartars, Bohemians, crusaders? They probably came to Spain from the Arab world and then arrived in Italy called by their Saracen name, *Nabi*.
This game of cards is evidently far removed from the spirit of the tarot. (Zick Januarius, eighteenth century, Musée de Treves).

Ace of Coins (Visconti-Sforza deck) is one of the most beneficent cards in the deck. It represents perfect success both materially and spiritually. It amplifies all the good aspects of neighboring cards and is an antidote to their ill effects.

As with the major arcana there exists an infinite variety of ways to read the cards. They can be laid out in a cross, as we have discussed earlier in regard to the major arcana, or in a row of seven. If the latter method is chosen, the first three cards represent the recent past, the central card the situation in question, the three final cards future developments.

In any event all the methods used for the major arcana can be adapted for the minor arcana. Sometimes, when using only the latter, most interesting results can be obtained by arranging them in a zodiacal circle. Cards will be placed in each house to reflect various aspects of our situation.

Once again here are the significations of the twelve houses:

FIRST HOUSE...	The self, the interior life
SECOND HOUSE...	Gains and acquisitions
THIRD HOUSE...	Study, writing, brothers and sisters
FOURTH HOUSE...	One's roots, childhood, the father
FIFTH HOUSE...	Creation either of work or of children
SIXTH HOUSE...	Daily routines, minor illnesses
SEVENTH HOUSE...	Contracts, marriage, others
EIGHTH HOUSE...	Death, inheritance, sexuality
NINTH HOUSE...	Voyages, strangers, wisdom
TENTH HOUSE...	Ambition, success, the mother
ELEVENTH HOUSE...	Friends, joint undertakings
TWELFTH HOUSE...	Isolation, imprisonment, hospitalization but also the mystic path

One places three cards in each house. This will provide a detailed commentary on the various aspects of our situation.

It is possible and often desirable to use both major and minor arcana together in a reading. This will provide a fuller and more detailed understanding to the one seeking consultation.

(*Above*) The Ace of Staves (Visconti-Sforza deck), card of realization and invention, concerns only mentation and ideas. Again we find the family motto, "*A bon droyt.*" This was suggested to the first duke of Milan, Giangaleazzo Visconti, by the poet Petrarch.

(*Below*) The Ace of Cups (Visconti-Sforza deck) is a symbol of the grail that is perfection, it is overflowing love, which brings happiness, wealth, pleasure, and desire—a desire that is sane, constructive, and generous. It also represents domestic tranquility.

105

The Tarot as Seen by Artists and Poets

The macrocosm, the great world, is constructed by Kabbalistic arts; the microcosm, the little world, is its reflection in our hearts.

—Nerval

A Legion of Painters and Designers

From the beginning the tarot has been a favorite subject for artists. The deck created for the Visconti-Sforza family was executed by Bonifacio Bembo, a notable Cremonese painter of the thirteenth century.

Today, we think that the tarot cards we call the Mantegna deck, dating from around 1470, have been incorrectly attributed. They were probably the work of Parrasio Michele de Ferrare and provide a magisterial example of the art of engraving in Italy during this epoch. The style of these cards bears a strong resemblance to that of the frescoes at Schifanoia Palace, executed by Francesco Cossa.

Between 1496 and 1506 Albrecht Dürer, the celebrated painter and engraver, completed a set of twenty-one cards inspired by the Mantegna deck.

Most of the artists who painted or designed tarot decks between the Renaissance and the end of the last century have remained unknown, a fact that is paradoxical when one considers their large number. One ought, however, mention General Abner Doubleday, a painter in his leisure hours, who during the Civil War created drawings for a deck of tarot cards that he later colored by hand.

In the twentieth century a number of artists have emerged from anonymity. In 1910 an American member of the Order of the Golden Dawn, Pamela Colman Smith, painted a deck in the Art Nouveau style under the direction of Arthur Edward Waite. Guided by another and more famous member of the same order, Aleister Crowley, Lady Freda Harris, member of parliaments, painted a magnificent version of the cards. These were exhibited in London in 1942.

Contemporary painters have reproduced tarot decks in numerous genres. Marty Yeager, American surrealist, conceived of a set of cards designed for meditation. Peter Balin has created a tarot based on pre-Columbian costumes and beliefs. Gordon Chorprash's rendering of a tarot deck conceived by Morgan Robbins brings to mind Tibetan mysticism.

Two Italian painters, Domenico Balbi and Guido Bolzani, have provided us with highly original modern versions of the tarot. Peter Huckerby, and English cubist, illustrated his deck with black gouache. Also worthy of note is a deck created by Gianni Novak, another cubist painter, which was commissioned by Alitalia Airlines.

Taly-Price, whose portraits include some of the most celebrated figures of our time, has drawn a highly personal tarot. Her symbolism and coloring were guided by her own gifts as a medium.

Salvador Dali, whose artistic genius is equaled only by his taste for the dramatic, has put his fantastic and delirious imagination at the service of the traditional symbolism of the tarot, painting a remarkable deck for his wife, Gaia, a passionate devotee of mysticism.

Poets Respond to Call of the Tarot

That numerous poets have been fascinated by the tarot should not surprise us: Are they not often visionaries, sensitive to the occult, entranced by symbols, colors, and celestial things?

In the *Inferno*, Dante speaks of "great shards of fire" that fell from the sky, as in the Tower. He also takes up the themes of Judgment and the Wheel of Fortune.

At the end of the fifteenth century, Matteo Maria Boiardo, author of *Roland Amoreux*, interpreted the tarot in a cycle of seventy-eight terza, one for each card.

L'Aretin, in 1540, gave his own personal interpretation of each card. During the same period, a poem by Bertoni related tarot cards to women in the court of Isabella d'Este. Rabelais listed the "tarau" as one of the games that Gargantua was skilled in.

(*Opposite*) The High Priestess as seen by Taly-Brice, portraitist who has painted numerous celebrated men and women of our time. She has created a new form for this card, which she calls Science: She is the guardian of the door that leads to the sanctuary of consciousness.

The 7 of Staves (Hanson-Roberts, a reinterpretation of the Rider-Waite deck) announces a sudden influx of money, sometimes from gambling. It counsels swift action while the time is propitious.

More recently Gerard Nerval attached a particular importance to the Star, which runs through all his work. This card corresponds to the number 17, which is the numerological transcription of the year of his birth, 1808. Nerval belonged to a neo-Pythagorean tradition. For him, numbers and names had powerful significance. He had given himself a number of pseudonyms before arriving at the one by which he is known today. He was also greatly indebted to the occultists Court de Gibelin and Fabre d'Olivet, who had brought Pythagorean doctrines to the attention of the public at the end of the eighteenth century.

All his heroines are messengers: Sylvie brings to mind the Druids, which so fascinated Nerval; Celenie is Selene, the Moon, eighteenth card of the major arcana, identified with Artemis, chaste huntress, who also plays a large part in his work, particularly *Promenades et Souvenirs*. Isis personifies the mother-goddess, and also the unconscious, the interior world that goes beyond the limits of the separate personality. Isis is also the mother that the writer never knew. His died while he was still very young. On his quest to find his mother, once again, Nerval identified himself with Lucius, hero and initiate in Apuleius's *Golden Ass*. Lucius's history, his return to the land of his mother, describes the journey of man toward the spiritual life.

In *Aurelia*, Nerval considers the relation of the macrocosm and the microcosm. Cosmogony fascinated him. He spoke of the continuous interplay among all created things: "Everything is alive, everything is moving, everything corresponds . . . the choir of stars participates in my joys and sorrows. . . ." His imagery returns time and again to the redemptive star and to water as source of regeneration. He often quotes the Swedish visionary Swedenborg, and the Count of Saint-Germain, an initiate who claimed to have lived for hundreds of years; he also speaks to us of past lives.

Nerval's work has many clear references to the tarot. When he writes, "Mortals have to come to cast away all hope and prestige; and raising your sacred veil, O Goddess, the bravest of your adepts finds himself face to face with death," it is hard not to think of the High Priestess who leads us by secret pathways to Death.

In his *Les Chimères* the poem entitled *"El desdichado"* (The Disinherited) speaks of several of the major arcana:

> I am darkness—the widow—the unconsoled
> The prince of Aquitaine in his crumbling tower
> My star is dead, and
> Bears melancholy's black sun.

Here are obvious references to the Tower, the Star, and the Sun. A little further on he refers to Death:

> The thirteenth returns . . . Once again the first
> And it is always alone—
> It is death—or the dead—O exquisite torment.

In *Arcane 17*, André Breton describes in his turn the Star from the tarot of Marseille, remarking on alternate yellow and red stars that sparkle, the young girl who tips her two vases on the water, with her back turned to the thorn tree. Breton also makes reference to Fabre d'Olivet, Swedenborg, Eliphas Levi, and Nerval, who served to guide him back to Pythagoras. For Breton, the Star represents spiritual radiance.

The Tarot, Mirror of the Soul

We have the inherent capacity to become that which we desire.
—Pico della Mirandolla

The tarot is anthropocentric; the arcana force us to turn within, faced by the trials of earthly existence and our ignorance of what the future holds for us.

Pythagoras has taught us that we can only submit to the dictates of fate. If we can accept them without revolt, not in a spirit of resignation and passivity, but with the awareness that we can learn from our experiences and benefit from those events that, while they are happening, are the most difficult to bear, we can progress on the road of life. This progress is enacted as much on the physical and material plane as on the spiritual. Once we pass through these trials, they can be the occasions for important changes and new significant directions that will make our lives more agreeable.

As long as our perception of the world is fragmentary, as long as we consider ourselves as apart from our environment, we are stuck in an egotistical illusion and think the world revolves around us. But the universe is a continous process of dynamic exchange between the observer and the observed.

Oriental religions teach us that our fundamental objective should be to become aware of the unity underlying all phenomena, to see the world as constant interaction, to go beyond the idea of the isolated individual to identify ourselves with cosmic reality. As soon as we realize that all our personal actions are related to the play of universal forces, we feel ourselves freed from the chains that bind our thought and imagination.

Scientific experimentation has confirmed, in the words of Niels Bohr, "the indivisibility of all things." Subatomic particles, brought together for a time and forcibly separated, behave after this separation as if they were still dependent on one another. Each seems to "know" what the other is doing, even when they are separated by vast distances.

Man is faced with the task of overcoming his limitations to arrive at the truth. It is impossible to arrive at the source of being solely by the exercise of reason.

Saint Augustine, examining his own existence, said, "I believe that I exist; I could be wrong in believing this, but if I am then that is further proof of my existence, since for there to be an error, there must be a subject who errs. Thus whether my reasoning has foundation or not, my existence is assured." It is true that through his reason, man participates in Divinity. All thought is a kind of action, and matter interposes itself between thought and its realization. If one can overcome the inertia of matter, one can bring one's ideas into being. To get beyond this materiality, which often obscures what is right before our eyes, we have the need for additional impetus. Symbols are most efficacious in the pursuit. Wanting to encompass the unknown within the known we arrive at a stalemate. To understand the cosmic universe we must leave behind our limited perspectives.

Levi-Strauss describes the impasse our civilization finds itself in, by trying to describe all phenomena in strictly physical terms: "What I learned in effect, from listening to so many teachers, reading so extensively in philosophy, visiting different cultures and exploring the scientific tradition which is the pride and glory of Western civilization, simply leads me to what the sage seated beneath a tree discovered in meditation."

This brings us to modern science, particular physics, which in the twentieth century has finally arrived at demonstrating the truths taught by ancient religions. The observer is now seen to exercise an irrevocable effect on the phenomena observed. Bergson anticipated this understanding when he counseled that man would attain a far deeper comprehension if he were to abandon his disjunctive day-to-day thinking. All this echoes the Vedic teaching that separation is illusion. Man can elevate his consciousness; in so doing he gains knowledge of past, present, and future.

Having meditated on this life and the hereafter I have forgotten my fear of birth and death.

—Milarepa

Man and Anxiety

From the moment of birth, and even before, man's life is riddled with anxiety. In the womb, afloat in amniotic fluid, which evokes the primordial mother, the original soup out of which all life emerges, the child often feels the effects of the mother's anxieties. And this anxiety can only be intensified when the fetus is forced to depart from this place of well-being to be born into the world. Now he must submit to the indignities of the process of birth, the trauma of separation from the mother who nourished him and kept him warm, whose being he shared, to face all alone a hostile and cold world in which he is suddenly abandoned.

The recollection of this separation will never leave him, even if he arrives at some provisional equilibrium or succeeds in burying it deep in the unconscious. His entire life will be a quest for a lost paradise.

This primal anguish can only increase when he begins to interrogate himself about the origin and meaning of life. He senses himself in the grip of powerful forces whose ends are obscure. From the beginning of human history, we can discern traces of this anxiety in the face of the mysteries of the universe. It is not so far from the terror that must have seized Neanderthal man before the fury of unchained natural forces.

Augustine, Pascal, Kierkegaard, and many others have written at length about the consuming anguish inherent in the human condition. The nothingness of certain modern existentialism is nothing more than a way of escaping questions that have already been posed—a refusal to face questions that are impossible to answer.

In endless night, man hurls himself against a God that he does not comprehend. Since God does not reveal himself in mathematical theorems, no scientific method can prove his existence. Man does not want to die, to become shrouded in an infinity of nothingness. Despite its vicissitudes, life is sweet. As Nietzsche has written, "All pleasure longs for eternity."

This still life combines several of life's pleasures—reading, music, cards—while reminding us that the voyage ends in death. For this reason the genre it belongs to is named "vanity." (Anonymous, seventeenth century, Musée de Louvre)

111

112

From the Unreal lead me to the Real
From Darkness lead me to the Light
From Death lead me to Immortality
—*Upanishad Brihad—Aranyaka*

Remembrance of Oneself

Before studying to read the tarot cards, it is as important to reject certain assumptions as to clarify others. First of all, we must recognize that no one card is more important than another. Certain cards yield their signification more easily, but all are of equal value. As with human beings, their meanings exist in their relationships to others.

The rituals that have grown up around the cards envelop them in mystery, lend them a superficial and theoretical weight, but are in truth not essential. You can arrange them in any fashion, decorate them as you wish; they will speak to you to the extent that you are able to listen to them and understand their symbolism. It is, however, evident that they ought to be respected and protected from dirt and wear and tear. Wrap them in whatever color you please—it need not be the violet of initiation or the white of purity. You might prefer to make for them a container of leather or wood or another suitable material.

You can consult them Wednesday, Sunday, or Monday, the beginning of the month or the end, night or day, as often as you care to.

The tarot will respond to the inner questions that you pose even if you have not fully formulated them. In the *Pensées* Pascal remarks, "Man does not know where he belongs. He is visibly lost, fallen from his true estate without the power to return. With an uneasy heart he searches everywhere, without success in unpenetrable darkness." The tarot helps man to regain "his true estate" his proper place, first in relation to others and finally to the cosmos. The tarot awakens man to his own consciousness, and this is the first step toward rejoining the divine consciousness. It shows him how to leave the prison of his limited nature and arrive at a higher level of awareness. The light of the past dispels the darkness of the future, and the future will in its time become memory.

The symbolism of the tarot is more efficacious than any explanation. Imagery speaks more directly to us than words. When one has assimilated a book on symbolism such as the tarot, do not, as Gide counsels in *Les Nourritures terrestres*, throw it away, but put it away with care, keeping only a memory that will enable you to arrive little by little at your own understanding. To end by paraphrasing Gide once more, let us hope that it teaches you to become more interested in yourself than in it, and then more interested in others than in yourself.

(*Opposite*) Young, independent, precocious, sometimes boastful, the Page of Staves (Visconti-Sforza deck) may be of foreign extraction or may live abroad. He carries a joyful message and is himself a figure of dynamic energy. Good news follows him.

(*Above*) The 6 of Hearts of the great deck of Mademoiselle Lenormand: Protected by a powerful man practiced in the alchemical arts, the male consultant is pictured (*lower left*) making a match to his advantage; the female consultant (*lower right*) is being wooed by a highly placed individual.

Divinations and Celebrated Prophecies from Legend and History

It is just the same with prophecies, miracles, divinations by dreams, lots, etc. Because if there was no truth to any of them no one would have ever believed in them: and thus, rather than concluding that there are no true miracles because there are so many false ones, one must see, on the contrary, that there are certainly true miracles since there are so many false ones and that false ones exist for this reason; that there are indeed true ones.

—Pascal, Pensées

The tarot is simply one method of prognostication among others. The future, which is inscribed in the past, has been predicted by a variety of methods from the mists of antiquity to our day. All throughout human history one sees confirmation of the prophecies of past seers.

The Oracles of Antiquity

All the people of antiquity had among them wise men who interpreted the signs of heaven. Consultations were given in exchange for gifts offered by the petitioners. Certain divines were in the service of kings: The Bible reports that Gad and Nathan officiated in the court of Daniel, and the great prophet Samuel also acted as counselor for the king. The old Testament is filled with accounts of the activities and sayings of the great prophets of the Hebrews.

Dodona and Delphi: High Place of the Oracles

Archaelogists have uncovered tablets on which are engraved simple questions posed by inhabitants of Dodona in Epitus to the oracle of Zeus and Diana, one of the earliest oracles in Greece. It is well known how important these divine responses were to the ancients and the significant role they played in political life.

Cicero, a true skeptic, declared that the Delphic oracle could not have preserved its reputation through the ages if its predictions did not come true. Croesus, the king whose fabled wealth still lives on in our everyday language in the expression "as rich as Croesus," followed the instructions of the oracles to the letter. Thucydides, the eminent Greek historian, reports a pronouncement of the oracle predicting that a plague would break out if the Spartans invaded Athenian territory. The oracle proved correct in every detail.

Divination During the Renaissance

Nostradamus

Before he had changed his given name to Nostradamus (a play on words meaning "we give that which belongs to us"), Michel de Notredame accosted an unknown monk on a road in Savoy and knelt before him. The monk was completedy astonished. Nostradamus said to him: "But this is how one is supposed to act in the presence of your holiness." The unknown monk was named Felix Peretti. He was destined to become Pope Sixtus V.

Everyone knows that Nostradamus warned Catherine di Medici not let her husband engage in single combat in an enclosed field in his forty-first year, or he would receive a severe head wound that could prove mortal. This prediction was confirmed by a celebrated Italian astrologer, Luca Gaurico. The queen tried desperately to prevent her husband, Henry, from dueling with Montgomery. But the king refused to listen and lost his life. He was forty-one years old.

In 1560 Antoine Couillard published a pamphlet entitled "In Contradiction of Nostradamus," that attempted to ridicule the seer for, among other things, predicting

(*Opposite*) Justice (deck of Charles VI) evokes order, governance, right rule. It is the law of cause and effect; it rebukes us for our faults and rewards our generous deeds. It is a card of equilibrium but also of rigor and severity.

"an exceptional conjunction of forces and revolution for the year 1789." Ronsard took issue with his detractors and voiced in rhymes his estimation of the worth of his prophecies:

> As the prophets of old, he over the course of years
> Has predicted much of our destiny.

In Saon, Nostradamus encountered Henri de Navarre, who was at that time eleven years old, in the company of his tutor. Nostradamus is said to have told the tutor: "If you live long enough you will see your student become master of Navarre and France." When he became king, Henri often recounted this episode from his youth, which had made a powerful impression on him. However, years later when three magicians foretold that he would be assassinated while riding in a carriage, the king did nothing but laugh. Two days later, Ravaillac made that prophecy come true.

Paracelsus

The baron Theophrastus Bombast von Hohenheim, who later took the name Paracelsus, was born in 1493 in Einseidhem, near Zurich. Endowed with extraordinary intelligence, he spoke seven languages and is considered to be the father of modern medicine. He elicited the respect of Erasmus, Montaigne, and Francis Bacon. He also possessed a gift of divination, which was recognized by his contemporaries. During a trip to Sweden he claimed that there was gold beneath the snow between latitudes 63 and 65. In 1933, several centuries later, gold was discovered in Sweden at Bolendin, at 64.5 degrees, north latitude.

In his book *Prognostications*, published in Augsburg in 1536, Paracelsus predicted the fall of the French monarchy two and a half centuries before it actually happened.

But he was predated by a French prelate, Pierre d'Ailly, nicknamed "the eagle of the holy doctors of France." After studying various astrological conjunctions, this man foretold that tremendous political upheavals would occur in 1789.

Mother Shipton: English Clairvoyant

There appeared in 1641 in London an edition of a book of prophesies that had been made at the beginning of the sixteenth century. Popular tradition attributed them to Mother Shipton. Born in 1488 in Yorkshire, Ursula Southeil, wife of Toby Shipton, predicted the arrest and death of Cardinal Wolsey, the archbishop of York and Chancellor of the Realm, at the height of his glory. She foretold other tragic destinies as well—the deaths of the duke of Suffolk and Lord Percy and the military defeats of Lord Darcy. Her prophesies were written in a style peculiar to herself.

Her predictions include references to the automobile, airplane, submarine, tunnels, and telecommunications. It is clear that in the sixteenth century these could have only been considered the wildest imaginings.

A Prediction Related by Saint-Simon

The duke of Saint-Simon, who had nothing but contempt for magic and sorcery, recounted in his *Memoirs* an event that had made a strong impression on him and that was told to him by Philippe d'Orleans in 1706. A seer, whose name is not mentioned, predicted at that time the death of Louis XIV and named those who would surround his death bed.

The seer had made this prediction at a soirée held by the duke d'Orleans, in the presence of the playwright Adrienne Lecouvreur, Montesquieu, President Hénault, and Voltaire. To the great astonishment of the company, he declared that he did not see any members of the royal family near the dying king, neither Monseigneur, the dauphin, nor the king's grandson, the duke of Burgundy. He described, however, a little boy about five years old, guided by a servant.

Saint-Simon laughed on hearing the story, thinking it absurd that an unknown child would be present near the king at such a solemn moment and that all the princes of the blood royal would be absent. Phillippe added that, according to the seer, after that occurrence the same child would wear a crown that was not France's, England's, or Spain's.

Seers and astrologers of the eighteenth century

The court astrologer of Frederick the Great, king of Prussia, announced to him one day that a great soldier had just been born. The date was August 16, 1769, birthdate of Napoleon.

Cagliostro, alchemist and seer, predicted in 1785 that Louis XVI would lose his throne and die on the scaffold. He also predicted that Marie-Antoinette would be imprisoned and decapitated and that the princess of Lamballe would be attacked and killed on a street corner by four ruffians. This last came to pass in 1792, as foretold.

He also predicted that a Corsican would take up the crown that had fallen from the hands of Louis, that he would be chosen by the people, that he would be lord of many kingdoms, but that he would end his life ruined, imprisoned on an island. According to the marquis of Launay, the governor of the Bastille, Cagliostro,

Morgan's tarot. These monochromatic cards, drawn by Gordon Chorparsh, were created in the late 1960s by Morgan Robbins. Each card is meant to serve as a mirror in which is reflected the depths of the soul and hence can be used for meditation. Some of the cards, inspired by Tibetan mysticism, have definite links to the traditional major arcana, whereas other cards simply offer advice.

1

2

3

4

5

who was arrested and imprisoned in the Bastille, etched on the wall of his cell, with the aid of a nail, that it would be destroyed on July 14, 1789, and that grass would grow in its place.

The Famous Prophecy of Cazotte

Cazotte, the author of *Diable amoureux*, is responsible for a remarkable prophecy. His contemporary La Harpe reported it, in all its astonishing detail, in 1788 (one year before the French Revolution). Madame de Genlis provided additional confirmation, saying that she heard the story more than once, during this same period. Baroness Henriette Louise d'Oberkirch also speaks about it in her memoirs, completed in 1789. She asserts that she had heard about this prophecy in the winter of 1788–89 at the home of her friend, Monsieur de Puysegur, in Strasbourg. The English writer William Burt, in *Observations on the Curiosities of Nature*, relates that he was present when the prediction was made and heard it himself.

During the course of dinner given by the prince of Beauvau, who gathered around himself nobles of the court, writers, and intellectuals, among them Chamfort, Vicq d'Azyr, Bailly, Malesherbes, La Harpe, and the duchess of Gramont, there took place a lively political exchange. Advanced ideas about the state of society were put forward and more than one individual was heard to voice his approbation of revolution. Cazotte, who had not taken part in the discussion, suddenly announced in the most serious tone of voice that all of the company would witness the revolution, which they so desired, but that many would end up being killed in the name of that reason, liberty, and humanity that they were extolling. Their executioners would have on their lips the same lofty sentiments. He announced that Concordet would die in prison, poisoning himself to escape execution; that Chamfort would slit his wrists, linger for several months, and then die; that during the revolution Vicq d'Azyr would die from an attack of gout; that Bailly and Malesherbes would both die on the scaffold. The duchess of Gramont is said to have remarked that she rejoiced that ladies had nothing to fear, to which he responded that she would be led to the scaffold with princesses of the blood "and with many more noble women, all with their hands tied behind their backs." He added that only the king, who would also be executed, would be allowed to have a confessor at his side. Finally he predicted his own death. La Harpe, he added, would be spared by a miracle and, touched by grace, become a Christian. Though very shaken, the assembled party laughed at the thought of the freethinker La Harpe converting to Christianity.

Four years later, in 1792, the Reign of Terror installed itself in the name of Liberty and Reason. All those mentioned by Cazotte met their ends exactly as he had predicted. Cazotte himself, arrested August 10 and then released, let it be known that he did not have much time left. Arrested once again on September 11, he went to the guillotine two weeks later. La Harpe escaped the massacre and converted.

Several volumes would not suffice to list all the predictions made by clairvoyants that have been verified by succeeding events. World literature is filled with accounts of the fulfillment of startling, sometimes astonishing predictions. Many of the reporters have been great thinkers, writers, and philosophers. They note these remarkable events with surprise and admiration.

The examples cited above are meant to give the reader a general impression of the kinds of predictions that have been made about famous people. Those that addressed the destiny of ordinary men and women are most certainly vastly more numerous, but they remain forever shrouded in obscurity and disappear with their immediate witnesses.

Bibliography

L'Âne d'or, Marie-Louise von Franz, La Fontaine de pierre, 1981.
Arcane 17, André Breton, J.-J. Pauvert, 1971.
Bhagavad Gita, A.-M. Esnoul and D. Lacombe, Le Seuil (Points-sagesses 9), 1977.
Dictionnaire des symboles, J. Chevalier and A. Gheerbrant, Laffont (Bouquins), 1982.
The Encyclopedia of Tarot, Stuart R. Kaplan, U.S. Games Systems New York, 1978.
Hermès Trismégiste, trans. L. Ménard, Ed. de la Maisnie, 1979.
La Kabale des Kabales, Carlo Suarès, Adyar, 1962.
La Lettre, chemin de vie, A. de Souzenelle, Le Courrier du Livre, 1978.
Mythologie grecque et romaine, P. Commelin, Garnier (Biblio. Prestige), 1977.
Nerval, poète alchimiste, G. Lebreton, Curandera (Dedalus), 1982.
Œuvres, G. de Nerval, Garnier (Biblio. Prestige), 1978.
L'Or du millième matin, Armand Barbault, Flammarion (J'ai lu), 1972.
Le Phénomène humain, P. Teilhard de Chardin, Le Seuil (Points 6), 1970.
La Physique moderne et les pouvoirs de l'esprit, O. Costa de Beauregard, M. Cazenave and E. Noël, Le Hameau (Horizons Sciences), 1980.
Les Racines de la conscience, C.G. Jung, Buchet-Chastel, 1971.
La Science et l'âme du monde, Michel Cazenave, Imago, 1983.
Le Sepher yetsira, Carlo Suarès, Mont Blanc, 1970.
Les Spectrogrammes de l'alphabet hébreu, Carlo Suarès, Mont Blanc, 1973.
Tao tö king, Lao Tseu, Gallimard (Idées), 1969.
Le Tarot, A. Court de Gebelin, Berg. Int., 1983.
Le Tarot des imagiers du Moyen Age, Oswald Wirth, Laffont/Tchou, 1975.
La Théorie atomique et la description des phénomènes, Niels Bohr, Gauthier-Villars.
La Tragédie grecque, Guy Rachet, Payot, 1973.
Tristes Tropiques, Claude Lévi-Strauss, Presses Pocket (Terre humaine), 1984.
Six Upanishads majeurs, trans. from sanskrit by P. Lebail, Le Courrier du Livre, 1971.
Védisme et hindouisme, Anne-Marie Loth, Le Bas, 1981.
The Way of Kabbalah, Zev ben Shimon Halevi, Rider & Cie, U.K., 1980.

PHOTOGRAPHIC CREDITS

J.-L. Charmet: 33, 59, 61, 84, 91. Dagli Orti: 29, 44-45. Edimedia: 93, 103. Giraudon: 18-19, 75, 110-111; Lauros: 82-83. B.-P. Grimaud: 10, 12, 16, 17, 20, 24, 26, 28, 32, 34, 35, 40, 41, 42, 46, 47, 48, 49, 50, 52, 53, 54, 55, 62, 66, 68 (1, 2, 3, 4), 78, 79, 86-87, 98, 99, 113. Archives Nathan: 22, 30, 56, 77, 114. Taly-brice: 106. U.S. Games Systems: 51 (3), 73, 97 (2), 100 g, 108, 117.

ACKNOWLEDGEMENTS

The publisher wishes to thank Maison J.M. Simon (B.P. Grimaud) for allowing us to reproduce a number of tarot cards. Thanks go as well to Stuart R. Kaplan, President of U.S. Games Systems who has granted us permission to reproduce cards belonging to the Morgan tarot (© 1970) the Rider-Waite deck (© 1971) and that of Mary Hanson Roberts (© 1985).